EDITED BY
AL BAIRD AND WYNDHAM SHAW

CHURCH-BUILDING
ELDERSHIPS
Godly Qualities that Produce Great Churches

Church-Building Elderships

Al Baird and Wyndham Shaw, Editors
Copyright © 2019 by Al Baird

ISBN: 9781948450454.

Published by Illumination Publishers, 6010 Pinecreek Ridge Court, Spring, Texas 77379, (www.ipibooks.com).

All rights reserved. No part of this publication may be reproduced, stored in a retrieval system, or transmitted in any form or by any means—electronic, mechanical, digital, photocopy, recording, or any other—except for brief quotations in printed reviews, without the prior permission of the author and publisher.

Printed in the United States of America.

Illumination Publishers titles may be purchased in bulk for classroom instruction, business, fund-raising, or sales promotional use. For information, please e-mail paul at paul.ipibooks@me.com.

Illumination Publishers cares deeply about using renewable resources and uses recycled paper whenever possible.

All Scripture quotations, unless otherwise indicated, are from The Holy Bible, New International Version, Copyright © 1973, 1978, 1984, 2011 by Biblica, Inc. Used by permission. All rights reserved worldwide.

All Scriptures marked NKJV are from *The Holy Bible, New King James Version*. Copyright © 1982 by Thomas Nelson, Inc. All rights reserved.

Interior text layout by Toney Mulhollan and cover design by Roy Appelsamy of Toronto, Canada.

About the Authors

Al Baird serves as a full-time elder in the Phoenix Church of Christ. He was married for fifty-six years, but recently lost his beloved wife, Gloria. He has three daughters and nine grandchildren. He has been an elder for thirty-five years in three churches.

Ron Brumley serves as an elder in the San Diego Church of Christ. He has served as an elder for forty years in four different churches. He has been married to Linda for fifty-eight years and has four children and ten grandchildren. One of his sons was recently appointed an elder. Ron is a retired school principal.

John Brush has served as an elder in the South Florida Church of Christ for twenty years and currently serves as a full-time elder. He has been married to Pat for thirty-nine years and has two daughters and four grandchildren.

Larry Craig has served as a full-time elder in the New York City Church of Christ for twenty-two years. He has been married to Mary Lou for fifty years and has three children and nine grandchildren.

Israel Ereola has served as an elder in the Lagos Christian Church for twelve years. He has been married to Abigail for forty-five years and has nine children and twelve grandchildren. He is registrar for the West Africa School of Missions.

Walter Evans has served as an elder in the Greater Philadelphia Church of Christ for fourteen years. Married to Kim for thirty-five years, he has three children and four grandchildren. He serves as a full-time elder and has served as an evangelist in many churches for decades.

Darren Gauthier has been an elder in the Chicago Church of Christ for five years. He has been married to Sharon for twenty-eight years and has two children.

Bill Hooper has served as an elder in the Dallas/Ft. Worth Church of Christ for twenty-seven years. He has been married to Sally for fifty-two years and has three children and nine grandchildren. He is now retired from full-time ministry.

Frank Kim has served as an elder in the Denver Church of Christ for ten years, and as a missionary and evangelist for many years prior. He has been married to Erica for thirty-four years and has three daughters and four grandchildren. He is CEO of Pactimo, a cycling apparel company.

Sam Laing has served as an elder for eleven years and as an evangelist for many decades. He has been married to Geri for forty-seven years and has four children and eleven grandchildren. He currently lives in Myrtle Beach, South Carolina, serving as a teacher and author.

Dan Liu has served as an elder in the Hong Kong Church of Christ for eight years. He has been married to Elexa for twenty-nine years and has two sons. He works full-time for HOPE worldwide.

Dr. Mike Shapiro has served as an elder for ten years. He has been married to Mary for thirty-five years and has three children and four grandchildren. He currently lives in Apex, North Carolina, and works as a psychologist and director of behavioral medicine.

Wyndham Shaw has served as a full-time elder in the Boston Church of Christ for twenty-eight years and served as an evangelist there for thirty-three years. He has been married to Jeanie for forty-four years, has four children, and eight grandchildren. He is now retired, due to health challenges.

Jerry Sugarman has served as an elder in the Los Angeles Church of Christ for twenty-one years. He has been married to Erlyn for forty years. He has one son and two grandsons. He works as a dentist and full-time ministry volunteer.

Contents

Preface
Al Baird
— 7 —

Introduction
Wyndham Shaw
— 9 —

1. Elderships That Build Churches
   Wyndham Shaw
   — 13 —

2. Elders throughout History
   Al Baird
   — 21 —

3. A Biblical Vision of Elders
   Larry Craig
   — 27 —

4. Qualities and Qualifications of Elders
   John Brush
   — 33 —

5. The Heart of a Shepherd
   Bill Hooper and Dan Liu
   — 41 —

6. Companions in Leadership: Wisdom from Our Wives
   Twelve elders' wives
   — 51 —

7. Shared Leadership: Elders and Other Gifted Roles
   Frank Kim
   — 67 —

8. Elders as Family Builders in God's Church, Part 1
   Sam Laing
   — 77 —

Contents

9. Elders as Family Builders in God's Church, Part 2
   Sam Laing
   87

10. Working Dynamics of an Eldership
    Wyndham Shaw
    93

11. Guarding the Flock: Eldership Authority and Church Discipline
    Jerry Sugarman and Ron Brumley
    101

12. Every Effort for Unity
    Darren Gauthier, Israel Ereola, and Wyndham Shaw
    109

13. Elders as Peacemakers: Conflict Resolution
    Walter Evans
    121

14. Elders as Counselors: When Do We Recommend Professional Treatment?
    Dr. Mike Shapiro
    131

15. Elders as Learning Leaders
    Wyndham Shaw
    141

16. Shepherds Search for Lost Sheep
    Wyndham Shaw
    145

17. Eldership Appointments
    Al Baird and Wyndham Shaw
    151

Preface

Selecting godly elders marks a major stepping stone in the maturing of a church. Elder appointment should be a significant goal of every church and a cause for great rejoicing when it happens. Rich blessings come when elders oversee the church. One of the blessings is their example of family life. These men are to have exemplary marriages and God-focused children—they are not perfect in these areas, but worthy of respect. The leadership they provide is a living example, giving hope to disciples that they, too, can have godly families. Since these men have built healthy families, together they can help the church function as a healthy family. Another blessing is unity. Elders have the experience of building unity in their own families, and they have the authority to resolve conflict—maintaining peace and harmony in the church. Elders are a vital part of God's plan, not only as a part of his design for the health and growth of the local congregation where they serve, but as a part of the bigger plan of taking the good news of Jesus Christ to the lost world.

We have witnessed and rejoiced in the rapid numerical growth of the church, especially in the early years, and have prayed, strategized, and agonized over how best to help these young disciples grow up as healthy members of the body. A major part of the solution lies in training and raising up elders who can feed the flock. The number of elders has increased, but primarily in the United States. In 2010, when I turned seventy, Gloria and I decided we would turn our focus toward training men and women who could be elders and elders' wives outside of the borders of the United States. At that time there were only two or three elderships in other countries. Wyndham and Jeanie have shared the same vision. We thank God that there are now elderships in twelve other countries. Not nearly all that success is due to the Shaws and Bairds; rather, it is the result of the hard work of many other men and women—but mostly the grace of God. We rejoice over the progress, although most of the work lies ahead. Only ten percent of our churches have elderships today.

This book is a labor of love that has taken months to put together but many years of experience to write. Wyndham and I began discussing the idea for such a book several years ago. The idea caught fire with the Elders' Service Team, a group of twelve or so elders and their wives, and we all began writing it about twelve months ago. We are thankful for the contribution from Dr. Mike Shapiro, an elder and psychologist who contributed a needed chapter. A tremendous "thank you" goes to Jeanie Shaw for the many, many hours of work that she spent to brainstorm, create, edit, and harmonize the different writing styles of many authors—and who knows what else.

We pray that this book will be used by God to propel the inspiring work of raising up future elders.

—Al Baird
Phoenix, Arizona

INTRODUCTION
Wyndham Shaw

Church-building elderships do not just happen. They must be aimed for, developed, and trained. This was Paul's goal in his farewell meeting with the Ephesian elders (recorded in Acts 20) and in his instructions to Titus, the evangelist who appointed elders in numerous towns (Titus 1:5). Christ has a plan for his church, and part of that plan is leadership in local churches by godly men known as elders. Those who set their hearts on the eldership desire a "noble task" (1 Timothy 3:1). Churches who have godly elderships are blessed and should experience the fruits of such leadership. However, none of us will be inspiring elders or have church-building elderships without humility toward learning, and without a sincere effort to be mentored by those who have wisdom and experience.

This book is a compilation of the wisdom and experience of the elders who have been serving on the churchwide Elders' Service Team. Together, we have 516 years of experience as disciples, 263 of those while serving as elders.

The scene between Paul and the Ephesian elders in Acts 20 teaches us numerous lessons.

> When Paul had finished speaking, he knelt down with all of them and prayed. They all wept as they embraced him and kissed him. What grieved them most was his statement that they would never see his face again. Then they accompanied him to the ship. (Acts 20:36–38)

The most touching and inspiring part of this passage is not the qualities of the elders, or even their focus, but the love and relationships the leaders shared as they served the church. The elders wept because they would not see Paul's face again. He was beloved for his courage and caring. He was admired for his boldness in public and from house to house. It was his unconditional love and affection that brought them heart to heart.

He was not weak, but neither was he harsh; he was courageous and caring. Likewise, Paul was inspired by the courageous and caring lives of the elders. People follow courage and caring—not titles. Elders should be men who are appointed because of the life and inspiration they are already demonstrating—they don't do these things because of a title they are given.

Disciples today should see their elders as Paul saw his. When you have both courage and caring to hang in there with them for the long haul, it can and will produce a great affection. They will know you love enough to be there in their darkest hours and care enough to correct them in their sinful moments.

This book, while not exhaustive, is intended to touch on topics vital for growing as an elder and growing as an eldership (group of elders).

To this day, many speak of my late father-in-law and elder, Richard Whitehead, as the man of courage and caring who continues to inspire them forty-plus years after their conversion and many years after his death. I pray that the wisdom shared from the numerous elders in the pages of this book can motivate us to be inspiring shepherds in our churches as we follow the Chief Shepherd. Men of courage and caring are very rare. Let's become them, continue to be them, and support them!

> "Keep watch over yourselves and all the flock of which the Holy Spirit has made you overseers. Be shepherds of the church of God, which he bought with his own blood. I know that after I leave, savage wolves will come in among you and will not spare the flock. Even from your own number men will arise and distort the truth in order to draw away disciples after them. So be on your guard! Remember that for three

years I never stopped warning each of you night and day with tears.

"Now I commit you to God and to the word of his grace, which can build you up and give you an inheritance among all those who are sanctified." (Acts 20:28–32)

12

Chapter One

ELDERSHIPS THAT BUILD CHURCHES

Wyndham Shaw

I have known many inspiring elders in my life as a Christian. While none have been (or are) perfect, they all inspire me for the heart and faith they have embodied and the task of leadership they have embraced. We need more shepherds—not just in name or title but in heart, faith, and nobility before God.

As a young Christian, the first elder I ever met later became my father-in-law. My impression of this man, Richard Whitehead, was different from my view of my ministry leaders. He was an older man of stature and reputation. He taught the Bible class for college students, using more scriptures than I could keep up with in my note taking. He was affectionately nicknamed "the walking concordance." He even took some of us out for lunch after church and paid the bill! I was drawn to his public persona, which was bold, visionary, and Bible based. He demonstrated a positive exuberance and gave hugs that were known as "Brother Whitehead's kidney-chopper." To me, he was a tower of stability and maturity amid a rapidly changing cultural landscape in the world and the church.

I learned that he was a man of vision. He had left the church where his new bride's father was an elder to start a new church near the university campus. He desired to see the church grow—to build a church that would contain many campus students. My wife remembers him hanging a sign in the auditorium that read "500 in 5 years," a laughable goal for this tiny church. He then chartered busses to take church members to visit some of the fastest-growing congregations of the day to better learn how to build the church. He and his fellow elder sought to find the right leaders who could help the congregation to grow, and he had the courage to deal with trouble when it came. After I graduated and moved, the church grew to over 1200 members.

Shepherding and building God's church is not for the weak or fainthearted, but for the brave hearted. Shepherds like David were strong men of faith and courage who had soft hearts but demonstrated tough love and a genuine faith in God.

Ripe for Harvest

We live in an exciting and challenging time in the twenty-first century. We've experienced crisis in the world economy, terror attacks, and unsettling challenges for political leaders. However, there is no less a crisis in the spiritual realm—it is only less publicized. But with crisis comes opportunity for courage, faith, and leadership.

In our fellowship we have weathered a period of discipline and reactionary emotion and theology toward past mistakes. We face a defining moment, standing at a crossroads of choice about leadership models and leadership decisiveness. Our choice is to continue to build the church or to look back on it as a monument. Satan will always send threats within the church concerning sound doctrine about conversion, commitment, one-another responsibility, and evangelistic fervor. Church-building elders must rise up and respond if the church is to flourish.

Our world is ripe for harvest because of the fear (personal, relational, and financial) that is felt around the globe. God is using these ploughs of crises to cultivate a ripe harvest of the disillusioned who are looking for a new security. Workers are desperately needed to sow and reap in the harvest fields. Church leaders must cut through the confusion, fear, and complacency to sound a clear call for our churches to be the light of the world and salt of the earth Jesus intended his disciples to be.

In Acts 20, and again in 1 Timothy 5, elders are called by the Apostle Paul to oversee and direct the affairs of the church. Wherever they exist or wherever they are being raised up, overseers and shepherds must be prepared to provide leadership that glorifies God by meeting the crises of our world and our churches with conviction, faith, and courage. The crises in our world stem from man's separation from God and the proliferating sin that follows. The church is to be the bright beacon of light that shines in this dark world, helping more and more see the saving grace of Jesus and respond with trust, love, and obedience to his word.

Challenge or Opportunity?

Crisis always produces great challenge and great opportunity. Throughout the Old and New Testaments, elders continually call God's people to move forward in faith.

Historically, leaders within the world have called for boldness when there is temptation to retreat. Several of their quotes speak to the spirit needed in shepherd-leaders for such a time as this:

Sir William Wallace: "Men do not follow titles, they follow courage!" (spoken to men of noble position who did not have the faith or courage to inspire the nation in time of crisis).

Winston Churchill: "When you are going through hell, keep on going" (spoken when the British resolved to persevere as the bombing of London was wearing thin). Elderships must not compromise biblical convictions when they are painful to uphold and could lead to loss of leadership or membership.

Franklin Roosevelt: "The only thing we have to fear is fear itself" (spoken to move the hesitant American people toward the personal involvement and risk of World War II). The greatest challenge for most elder candidates is the task of calling disciples to the personal involvement of biblical discipleship—especially after specific extremes of the past that can lead to certain compromises of the present.

In a fictitious but relevant exchange from the movie *The American President,* an aide confronts the president with: "In the absence of genuine leadership, they'll listen to anyone who steps up to the microphone. They want leadership. They're so thirsty for it they'll crawl through the desert toward a mirage, and when they discover there's no water, they'll drink the sand." The president responds with: "People don't drink the sand because they're thirsty; they drink the sand because they don't know the difference!"

In our religious world, tainted by postmodern philosophy, knowing the difference between biblical living water and humanistic sand is a very real problem. We must have shepherds and elderships that know the difference and make sure that healthy biblical teaching and preaching is kept and supported in our pulpits and classes. This is crucial to building the church.

The decisions shepherds and church leadership teams make and the stands they take today will determine the future: the dream of thriving fellowships, or the nightmare of decline and discouragement in our churches.

Acts 20 paints an inspiring portrait of Paul's dream for vibrant churches and elderships in such a time as ours.

Paul, as he heads for Jerusalem, calls for the elders of the church in Ephesus, knowing this is his last opportunity before his death to set their vision for ministry and shepherding. Paul's words in 1 and 2 Timothy show his continued effort to influence this church through Timothy, a young evangelist. The leadership message to both is very similar. Biblical ministry that builds healthy churches is the model revealed by Jesus and made visible through the collective leadership of elders, evangelists, and teachers. This is plain to see as we study 1 and 2 Timothy and Titus (the Pastoral Epistles) and the vision for an elder's ministry set forth in Acts 20.

I recently had a discussion with a former minister who had powerfully preached the Word in the past. He was currently debating whether to follow Paul's ministry model or Jesus' ministry model. My conviction is that Paul's ministry is a progressive revelation of Jesus' ministry model. Jesus was not on earth or in the flesh when the new covenant church or lifestyle was in effect. The apostles were his plan to reveal the model for church life and leadership through their inspirational lifestyle and inspired writing.

The Importance of Vision

Before giving some biblical and practical specifics of shepherding, it should be stated that as young churches embark on elder development they must have an eldership vision. Elders are appointed by the Holy Spirit, but elderships are also forged and developed by men who allow the Spirit to mold and shape them personally and collectively. I have been a proponent of team leadership and have tried to implement it in my life and leadership since cowriting with Gordon Ferguson an elementary description of it in 2002 (*Golden Rule Leadership*). However, after promoting a consensus leadership style, we failed to give much definition to team decision making. Experience often leads to additional or edited chapters, and you can find them in Gordon's "sequel," *Dynamic Leadership.*

Through both my own experience and dialogue with many others, it remains clear that it is much easier to describe elements of team leadership than to practice them effectively! It is an art that takes both conceptual buy-in and learned skill sets to practice. Leadership teams (which are the closest thing younger churches have to elderships) that will oversee healthy and effective church growth must be built, developed, and grown through a deliberate vision, training process, and spirit of learning.

In Matthew 16:18, Jesus told Peter that upon this rock (Peter's confession that Jesus is the Messiah, the Son of the living God) he would build his church. This scripture is the first concept of church building in the New Testament and provides a vision for the role of elders and a vision on which to build the church.

This same concept is defined more clearly in Ephesians 4:11–16 where Paul, an expert church builder, says the apostles, prophets, evangelists, pastors, and teachers are gifts Jesus gave to build the church. Each gifted leadership role is essential to equip the saints and to mature the church. (It should be noted that since apostles were those who were eyewitnesses to Jesus, we have no reason to think this office continued after their deaths.)

The roles of elders and evangelists have often been viewed as being in competition with each other, but I believe they are intended to be two components of a team (alongside the teachers) that works together in building the church. I believe we also need to include counsel from wise women who help support the team and are often part of leadership groups.

Acts 20, 1 and 2 Timothy, and Titus are examples of Paul's instructions to a group of elders and to a young evangelist whose assignment is to appoint elders. Many of the same qualities of leadership are called for in each role.

Protection, Connection, Correction, Direction, Affection

It's important to note that the first church leaders had parallel vision. In Acts 20, the elders were given the charge to follow up with Paul's ministry. This ministry might be defined in five words: Protection. Connection. Correction. Direction. Affection.

Protection: The charge Paul gives the elders is to be on their guard against false teaching from within and without. Attackers of the church are described as ferocious wolves. Titus, in his letter from Paul, was told to appoint elders who would silence those who were disrupting whole households. So here we see elders and evangelists working together to protect the church.

Connection: Jesus, as the Chief Shepherd, tells us he knows his sheep by name and his sheep know him; they know his voice (John 10:2–5). The eldership is not a "job." To lead, we must gain a connection with the church that comes from conversations, caring about them, and creating safety so they can share what is in their heart of hearts.

Correction: In Acts 20, the elders are charged to imitate Paul's lifestyle of proclaiming the whole will of God without hesitation—publicly and from house to house. This implies that correction of lifestyles not in harmony with the written Word was part of their task. Paul's example was to be followed by both the elders and the evangelists. Leaders must be willing to confront sinful lifestyles in the church.

Direction: The elders in Acts 20 are entrusted with the word of God's grace to build up the church. The content that Paul wrote to the churches is intended to instruct on how God's people ought to live in every area of life. In other words, the direction of their life is intended to be biblical—from marriage, to parenting, to relationships and treatment of one another in social and legal matters, to the reality of death and dying. Convictions about core biblical values of church building must not only be shared among the elders, but also shared and expected with the members in keeping with such teachings as in Matthew 28:18–20 (world missions and discipling ministry); Ephesians 4:11–12 (gifted leadership roles to equip saints for the work of ministry), 1 Timothy 3:14–15 (membership expectations in the household of God); Acts 2:42 (devotion to the basics); and Galatians 2:10 (remembering the poor). Evangelism and prayer are fundamental parts of the lifestyle and direction of the church.

The word of his grace speaks to every area of life. Church-building elderships systematically seek to model, monitor, and address all areas and speak to whatever is the need of the hour.

Affection: In Acts 20 Paul concludes his direction to the elders with his and their tears in anticipation of his departure. This scene makes it clear that there was deep affection between them—as should be the case between the elders, the other leaders, and the members they oversee. Affection needs to be demonstrated as the elders see the pain or the celebrations of life in the membership. They are not to be stoically set apart by their position, but emotionally connected and attached because of their love. Paul's example of this can be seen in the affection he expresses in all his letters—expressions of love. Elders who aren't attached to their sheep are lacking a vital ingredient in building the church. Tears and expressions of love should be visible publicly and from house to house.

Acts 20 sets a vision of a church-building eldership modeled after the Apostle Paul and embodied by the elders he desired to see appointed. It takes time to become biblical shepherds who practice "love with skin on it." It takes perseverance and endurance to stay this way to the end. It takes humility to confess, repent of, and change mistakes and poor judgment—and courage to stand up and lead again with conviction and without hesitation. May we be these humble, courageous, and persevering elders whom God can use to build his church.

Chapter Two

ELDERS THROUGHOUT HISTORY

Al Baird

Elders have been around for a long time. While this statement can be taken several ways, in this chapter we will explore elders throughout history. The word "elder," or its equivalent in other languages, has been used in different countries and cultures to indicate a position of respect, honor, and authority throughout recorded history. This usage usually results from the idea that the oldest members of any given group are the wisest and thus the most qualified to rule, to provide counsel, or to serve their group in some other way.

History of the Word "Elder"

The word "elder" is most often translated in the Old Testament from the Hebrew word *zaqen,* referring to an aged man, but is most often used to describe a more specific role. In the Old Testament an elder was an elderly man who exercised authority or held a judicial office. Hebrew elders first emerged from the ancient patriarchal family institution. In Moses' time their office was firmly established, and they are mentioned as a matter of fact—continuing to serve as local leaders throughout the entire Old Testament period.

As a social institution, various types of elders are named: elders of a people (Israel–Exodus 3:16; Moab and Midian–Numbers 22:7); elders of an area (Gilead–Judges 11:5); elders of tribes (Deuteronomy 31:28); elders of the exile (Jeremiah 29:1); elders of a city (2 Kings 23:1). The most prominent are elders of a people, a country, or a city.

The first mention of a body of elders among God's people is in Exodus 3:16 and 18 when God speaks to Moses out of the burning bush, commanding him to go to Egypt, speak to Pharaoh, and work to free the Israelites. God told Moses to let the elders know that God called him, and them, to this work. We do not know how or when this body of elders came to be, but it is significant that they existed before Israel was officially organized as a nation at Mount Sinai. By Exodus 24, a team of seventy elders had been selected as the governing body of Israel under the leadership of Moses.

From the burning bush calling onward, Moses worked closely with the elders. He taught them how to celebrate the Passover (Exodus 12:21), had them witness the miracle of water from the rock (Exodus 17:5–6), and took them with him up Mount Sinai where they "saw the God of Israel" (Exodus 24:9–11). When Moses went to Dathan and Abiram to pronounce God's judgment on these men, the elders were with him (Numbers 16:25). When Moses told God that he could no longer bear the burden of leading the people alone, God told him to assemble the elders so that he could commission and empower them to help Moses lead (Numbers 11:16–17). Elders served in the capacity of local magistrates and as governors over the tribes, having received detailed instruction regarding how to administer the law in the case of: one who intentionally killed another and fled to a city of refuge (Deuteronomy 19:11–13); unsolved murders (Deuteronomy 21:1–9); stubborn and rebellious children who did not turn from their way although chastened by their parents (Deuteronomy 21:18–21); a husband who alleged that his wife was not a virgin at the time of their marriage (Deuteronomy 22:13–21); the case of a man who refused to marry his brother's widow in order to raise up children for his brother (Deuteronomy 25:5–10; Ruth 4:1–12); and many other situations.

Role and Influence in the Old Testament

Elders' role and influence continued throughout the times of the Judges, the united and divided kingdoms, the Babylonian captivity and the return to the Promised Land. Righteous elders were of great importance in keeping the nation faithful to God. Joshua 24:31 and Judges 2:7 tell us that Israel served God all the days of Joshua (and of the elders that outlived Joshua who had personally witnessed God's miracles). The elders called Jephthah to be a judge to lead the people in the fight against the Ammonites (Judges 11:4–11).

King Saul, who had just been dethroned because of his sin, asked to be honored before the elders before he was removed (1 Samuel 15:30). Elders anointed David to take Saul's place as king over all Israel (2 Samuel 5:3). The new king Rehoboam foolishly rejected the advice of the elders (1 Kings 12:8), resulting in a divided kingdom and the eventual loss of most of the nation of Israel. Even the powerful king Ahab had to consult the elders of the land before proclaiming war (1 Kings 20:1–8). When the Jews returned from captivity, the power of the office of elder is again seen in the book of Ezra, as the elders of the Jews led the way in rebuilding the temple (Ezra 6:14).

However, their influence and actions were not always pleasing to God, as when they challenged Samuel to appoint a king to lead Israel rather than be led by God's prophet (1 Samuel 8:4–5) and when they took sides with Absalom against David in 2 Samuel 17:1–4. By the time of the Babylonian captivity the prophets scathingly rebuked the elders, as in Ezekiel 8:12.

Amid the times of the Babylonian captivity and the birth of Christ, when Israel was no longer a nation, and when the elders no longer had any civil authority, Jewish society began to function in synagogues. We do not read of them explicitly in the Old Testament, yet by Jesus' birth they were well-established institutions. As rulers of the synagogues, the elders then, like elders in the church today, oversaw the worship and spiritual lives of the people. Interestingly, there was always a plurality of elders in any synagogue. In addition to the synagogues, the most powerful Jewish ruling body (although not very powerful, because the Jews were under Roman rule) was the Sanhedrin, which was made up of seventy-one men—elders, former high priests, scribes, Pharisees, and Sadducees. This is the group that opposed Jesus and the early church. It was abolished when Jerusalem was destroyed in AD 70.

Elders in the New Testament

The role of elder in the New Testament church is more fully understood when we understand the roles of the Old Testament elders. The first Christians were Jewish, and the office was familiar to them. It follows that Luke did not need to explain his first reference to Christian elders in Acts 11:30. With respect to the duties of an elder, there is a continuity with the basic tasks of the elders in the Old Testament. All elders have the responsibilities of oversight and discipline of the congregation (Acts 20:28), and all are to rule and guide the people of God with the Word in a manner that is pleasing to God (Acts 20:29–31). Individual elders, such as James, had a significant role in the Jerusalem church and the Council of Jerusalem (Acts 11:30; 15:2–6, 22–23; 16:4; 21:18). Paul and Barnabas appointed elders (Acts 14:23, in reference to churches in Antioch, Pisidia, Iconium, Lystra, and Derbe) as a key step in organizing a new church. Paul then instructed Titus to appoint other elders (Titus 1:5). Paul spoke directly to elders in Acts (Acts 20:17) and warned them, "Keep watch over yourselves and all the flock of which the Holy Spirit has made you overseers. Be shepherds of the church of God, which he bought with his own blood" (Acts 20:28).

In the book of Revelation twenty-four elders sitting on twenty-four thrones surrounding the throne of God are mentioned. Whether this refers to Old Testament elders or New Testament elders or is figurative, as is much of Revelation, it does show the importance of the role of elders in God's overall design.

Whenever elders are mentioned in the New Testament, there is no inference of just one elder leading in any of the churches. They are referred to as *presbuteros* (elders) and *episkopos* (bishops) interchangeably. This was still the case later in the first century: the writings of the Apostolic Fathers (such as 1 Clement and the Didache) continue to assert the apostolic authority of the bishops/elders as rulers of the church, making no distinction between the two terms. But by the beginning of the second century, another of the Apostolic Fathers, Ignatius of Antioch, records that many churches had single bishops; this became the norm by the middle of the century. Ignatius distinguished between a bishop and elders, referring to the practice of a single bishop in a church, separated from the body of elders. Almost all Christian writers of the second century and later seem to have forgotten that there was ever a time when churches had multiple overseers.

As churches grew in size, those in smaller towns often did not have their own bishop. Instead, the bishop of the nearest large city would serve as overseer of the whole area. By the time of the Council of Nicea in AD 325, powerful bishops were leading large numbers of churches. By the fifth century, five bishops had risen to power overseeing much of the Christian world, and those five regions still exist today: Alexandria, Antioch, Constantinople, Russia, and Rome. Differences between the first four regions and Rome led to the "Great Schism" of 1054, resulting in the official existence of the Roman Catholic Church and the Eastern Orthodox Churches. The bishop of the Catholic Church took the title of Pope, and the bishops of the Orthodox Churches are called Patriarchs. Not only had the synonymous terms *presbuteros* (elders) and *episkopos* (bishops) taken on new and divergent meanings, but by the sixth century, presbuteros were functioning fully as priests in the sense that we think of the term today.

Straying from the Scriptures

Church government had been severely corrupted as Scripture lost its role as the guide for the church, its structure, and its practice. It was not until the Reformation began in 1517, with Martin Luther posting his Ninety-Five Theses, that significant attempts were made to return to the authority of the Bible. Reformers like Huldrych Zwingli and John Calvin studied New Testament church government and made major steps toward restoring the eldership. Calvin established a functioning eldership, teaching that like the early church, the eldership should consist of more than one elder.

An article entitled "Concerning the Elders," written in 1568 stated, "Each elder must diligently keep watch over his own parish or district, and visit the members under their care from house to house at least once a week, to instruct them and carry out spiritual oversight, as well as visit the sick."[1] Those churches adopting a "presbyterian" model abolished the office of bishop, and the leaders of local congregations began using the name "minister" instead of "priest." In this arrangement, the minister's leadership is shared with presbyters (also called elders). The Church of England retained Rome's form of church government—a hierarchy—but appointed the Archbishop of Canterbury

---

[1] Richard R. DeRidder, *Translation of Ecclesiastical Manual including the decisions of the Netherlands Synods and other significant matters relating to the government of churches*, by P. Biesterveld and H. H. Kuyper (Grand Rapids, MI: Calvin Theological Seminary, 1982), 30-32.

as the head of the church, in place of the pope. Other groups, such as Anglicans and Episcopalians, still follow this model. Some congregational and independent churches (including many Baptist churches) come closer to implementing the biblical form of church government, in that every congregation has an elder-like role. However, in such churches the office of elder or presbyter is usually found in the pastor only, while a board of deacons takes over much of the work that a body of elders should perform.

Elders and the Restoration Movement

The next significant series of events occurred in the early 1800s, primarily driven by an immigrant to America from Ireland named Alexander Campbell. The Reformation Movement that began in the 1500s attempted to "reform" the Catholic Church but resulted in many divergent beliefs and denominations. Campbell was adamant that all such divisions were ungodly and that the only solution was a complete return to the Bible for guidance and authority. Among the views and practices that Campbell championed were the independence of each local congregation; the rejection of all ministerial privileges without rejecting the ministry itself; the right and duty of laymen to have a part in leading the church; conversion involving faith, repentance, and immersion for the forgiveness of sins; weekly observance of the Lord's Supper; and a plurality of elders.

Unfortunately, what is now referred to as the Restoration Movement, which Campbell and others championed and through which our religious heritage flows, has fragmented into many separate groups—even though it began with the idea of uniting all of the denominations resulting from the Reformation Movement. Jesus' dying prayer in John 17 is for unity of believers, and one of Satan's most powerful (if not the most powerful) weapons is creating division. This, then, is one of the primary functions of elders today—to forge and maintain unity. May God help us have the vision, wisdom, and determination to fulfill this role—as well as all the others—as we serve and oversee his church as elders.

Chapter Three

A BIBLICAL VISION OF ELDERS

Larry Craig

Who are elders and why are they important in God's plan for the church? What does the Bible have to say about this role and its function? In this chapter we will seek to biblically answer these questions by asking who, what, when, where, and why.

1. <u>Who</u> Are the Elders of God's Church?

As mentioned in the previous chapter, the concept of older men who were responsible for guiding God's people was already in place when God sent Moses to deliver the Israelites. As God appeared to Moses in the burning bush, he told him to go back to Egypt and "assemble the elders of Israel" (Exodus 3:16; 4:29). References are made to the elders of Israel throughout the story of the exodus, the wandering in the desert, and the taking of Canaan. Nothing further is recorded about the qualifications of these men or how they were chosen. The peoples around what became the nation of Israel were also led by groups of men called elders, such as in the town of Sukkoth (Judges 8:14) in the time of Gideon and the elders of Gilead during the days of Jephthah (Judges 11:4–5).

As the history of the Jewish people continues in the Old Testament, there are always groups of leaders called elders, throughout the period of the judges, the time of the kings, the exile, and the return to Palestine. As Jesus begins his ministry, there is consistent reference to the elders. Again, there is no explanation or commentary on the specifics of their role or how they were appointed. However, they obviously had significant influence and authority over God's people.

It seems logical and appropriate that as the church was established God would institute a plan that had already been accepted by the Jews for hundreds of years. The first reference to elders as part of the new covenant is in Acts 11:30 when the church in Antioch sent famine relief "to the elders" of the church in Jerusalem.

As the New Testament reveals more about the qualifications and role of elders, the "who" becomes clearer. Just as in every instance in the Old Testament, in the New Testament the word is always in the plural form, "elders" (Acts 14:23, when Paul began appointing them, and Acts 20:17, when Paul met with the elders from the church in Ephesus). The men to assume this role were married men, mature enough to have believing children, and men of good character who were respected both inside and outside the church (1 Timothy 3:1–7; Titus 1:3–9). Paul even expressed that "whoever aspires to be an overseer desires a noble task" (1 Timothy 3:1), indicating that this was an admirable role. (More will be explained about the uses of other terms, like "overseer," to describe the function of elders.)

2. What Is the Elder's Role?

The elders in the Christian congregation are both shepherds and overseers:

> I exhort the elders among you…: shepherd the flock of God that is among you, exercising oversight, not under compulsion, but willingly. (1 Peter 5:1–2 ESV)

> Keep watch over yourselves and all the flock of which the Holy Spirit has made you overseers. Be shepherds of the church of God. (Acts 20:28)

Paul also speaks of elders directing the affairs of the church (1 Timothy 5:17). In the original Greek, the New Testament uses some terms interchangeably that in older English translations are rendered "presbyters" or "bishops." Most modern English translations use "elders" or "overseers." When Paul refers to "pastors" in Ephesians 4:11 he uses a word always translated as "shepherds" except in this place. It is generally believed that he is referring to the elder-shepherds. All these words indicate the responsibilities and function of biblical elders. Because of the pastoral nature of life in biblical times, people were aware of the role of shepherds to guide and protect the sheep. The church elders appear to have overseen the managerial aspects of the church as well as the spiritual welfare of the church and its members. More specifics of how they carried out their responsibilities are not given.

Another significant charge given to elders is to protect the church from false doctrine, which even in the early days of the church threatened to weaken the faith or cause the abandonment of God's plan and purpose. Paul instructed Titus to appoint men as elders who were sound in the faith.

> He must hold firmly to the trustworthy message as it has been taught, so that he can encourage others by sound doctrine and refute those who oppose it. (Titus 1:9)

It seems apparent that the elders have authority over the church, yet Peter admonishes them not to be "lording it over those entrusted to you, but being examples to the flock" (1 Peter 5:3).

3. When Were Elders Appointed or Recognized?

As mentioned earlier, in the Old Testament it is not revealed exactly how elders were appointed. Clearer examples can be seen in the New Testament church. After Paul had established congregations, he determined to revisit them to appoint elders in each one (Acts 14:23). Paul later wrote to Timothy about the kind of men who should be elders, and then charged Titus to appoint elders (1 Timothy 3:1ff; Titus 1:5).

There is no example shown of exactly how this process took place. Did the congregation recommend or select elders based on the guidelines Paul gave about character and maturity? Did the evangelists generally choose the men? No record is given of the congregation voting on elders, but they were vetted in some way by the church. No clear pattern is found. Certainly, the Holy Spirit could have given more specific instructions if that were necessary. The book of Leviticus, for example, shows God's will to give very specific directives about various situations. In absence of specific instructions, it would seem that congregations and evangelists can determine the best selection process. Since Paul told the Ephesian elders that the Holy Spirit makes overseers (Acts 20:28), we assume that congregations were officially recognizing men who were already known for their shepherding hearts.

There is also biblical basis for some elders being supported by the church:

> The elders who direct the affairs of the church well are worthy of double honor, especially those whose work is preaching and teaching. For Scripture says, "Do not muzzle the ox while it is treading out the grain," and "The worker deserves his wages." (1 Timothy 5:17–18)

Since elders are required to have children who are believers, it may take a while for some congregations to have qualified men. As congregations mature, more men become available to serve as shepherds by whatever method the church decides to identify them.

4. <u>Where</u> Do Elders Serve?

Paul returned to the places where he had preached and "appointed elders for them in each church" (Acts 14:23). He later had an emotional and heartfelt meeting with the elders of the church in Ephesus (Acts 20:17–38). Church history indicates that gradually one elder began to take a lead role over the other elders around him and then eventually over several churches. This pattern does not exist in the New Testament. Certainly, different men have different gifts, backgrounds, and opportunities, but biblical elders seemed to work together in humility, shepherding and overseeing the local congregation. We find instances of geographic regions of churches working together, such as in the collection of famine relief for the churches of Judea, but no group of elders appears to have oversight of another congregation outside of where they lived. Certainly the apostles and other church founders visited young churches they had started in order to help them grow. When churches are young, wisdom would suggest that they may need shepherding from sponsoring congregations, but each mature congregation is directed by its local elders. While this is the elders' main focus, we do see examples, such as the council in Jerusalem discussed in Acts 15, in which some of the more experienced elders were called upon to engage at the brotherhood level.

5. Why Are Elders Important?

The New Testament teaches that Jesus is our Chief Shepherd (John 10:10–18; Hebrews 13:20–21; 1 Peter 5:4); however, throughout history God's people have always needed flesh-and-blood leadership. The book of Judges recounts an unfortunate cycle. People more readily served and obeyed God when they had the godly leadership of a judge. When a judge died the people often reverted to disobedience and idolatry. During the days of the kings the spirituality of the nation (and then the two nations after the kingdom split) generally reflected the spirituality of the reigning king. Good leadership is imperative. Even though people are individually accountable to God, the collective body of God's people often drifts away without spiritual leadership. God's plan in his church is that elders provide this spiritual leadership to help his people stay faithful and obedient.

For this reason, elders are to be men of good character, seasoned and tested, and men who have been proven in their families so that they can take care of the people and manage the household of God effectively (1 Timothy 3:5). Elders provide maturity and stability for the church when the affairs of the church are handled righteously, prudently, and faithfully. Elders refute false doctrine. They are examples of devoted Christian living and help the church mature.

> So Christ himself gave the apostles, the prophets, the evangelists, the pastors and teachers, to equip his people for works of service, so that the body of Christ may be built up until we all reach unity in the faith and in the knowledge of the Son of God and become mature, attaining to the whole measure of the fullness of Christ.
>
> Then we will no longer be infants, tossed back and forth by the waves, and blown here and there by every wind of

teaching and by the cunning and craftiness of people in their deceitful scheming. Instead, speaking the truth in love, we will grow to become in every respect the mature body of him who is the head, that is, Christ. From him the whole body, joined and held together by every supporting ligament, grows and builds itself up in love, as each part does its work. (Ephesians 4:11–16)

Conclusion

Who are elders? They are spiritually mature men of noble character who are respected by everyone around them.

What is their role? They are shepherds and overseers, directing the affairs of the church.

When do they serve? They are appointed as they meet the qualifications and guidelines Paul expressed to both Titus and Timothy.

Where do they serve? The example in the New Testament is that men serve in their local churches, though at times they might serve the brotherhood as needed.

Why are they needed? Elders provide maturity, promote spiritual stability and growth, and keep the church sound in the faith.

May many more men desire the role of elder and prepare themselves to serve God's people, thus helping the church attain to the whole measure of the fullness of Christ.

Chapter Four

QUALITIES AND QUALIFICATIONS OF ELDERS

John Brush

The role of an elder is often multifaceted. As shepherds and overseers, these men must be high in character and spiritual maturity. Wisdom, which only comes with time and experience as a Christian, is necessary to function in this role, which is much more than one of simply natural talent. Spirituality and maturity are necessary in order for God to use these men to guide and protect his people. God has provided the model for church leadership in the New Testament, so it is natural and essential to ask the question, who should be appointed to this position?

Basic Qualifications of an Elder

The first question we would ask is: What kind of man should be considered for the office of elder in our congregations?

Paul and Peter instructed the churches of their day to seek as elders men who fulfill the qualities enumerated in 1 Timothy 3:1–7, Titus 1:5–9, and 1 Peter 5:1–4. It is interesting to note that the lists differ slightly, as different words are used to describe the same concepts. Paul did not give exactly the same list to the Ephesian church (under Timothy's leadership) that he did to Titus concerning the various churches he served, including Crete. Peter only listed a few qualities in his letter written to the churches scattered by the persecution. Paul and Peter did not have a "checklist" to give to the churches. Together, the combined list of all three passages gives us a clearer picture of an elder. All are slightly different views, giving us a more complete image. We have compared the qualities mentioned in the verses in the following table.

1 Timothy 3:1–7	Titus 1:5–9
Above reproach, well thought of by outsiders	Blameless
Faithful to his wife (or husband of but one wife: a "one-woman man")	Faithful to his wife (or husband of but one wife: a "one-woman man")
Temperate	Not quick-tempered
Self-controlled	Self-controlled, disciplined
Respectable	Upright
Hospitable	Hospitable
Able to teach	Holds firmly to the message; able to refute those who oppose sound doctrine
Not given to drunkenness	Not given to drunkenness
Not violent but gentle	Not violent
Not quarrelsome	Not overbearing
Not a lover of money	Not pursuing dishonest gain
Must manage his family well; children obey him out of full	Children believe and are not open to the charge of being wild and disobedient
	Loves what is good
	Holy
Not a recent convert	

(1 Peter 5:1–3 adds that elders must be willing to serve, not greedy for money, and not lording it over the flock but instead serving as examples to the flock.)

We can be apt to see these qualifications as a mere checklist. There is a strong tendency for this because we can be tempted to love rules rather than gleaning the character of the heart. What the Holy Spirit seems to be giving us here are two slightly different ways to view the character of the same man.

As we select elders in our churches it is helpful to recognize the influence handed down to us (largely from the Churches of Christ) concerning the way we search for and appoint the men to fulfill this office. We have traditionally taken a more literal interpretation or "conservative" approach to this process, where each quality in each list must be fulfilled. One example of this is the quality found in Titus 1:6. Titus says that the children must "believe," whereas 1 Timothy 3:4 merely says that he must "see that his children obey him, and he must do so in a manner worthy of full respect." This approach has limited the selection of elders to men who have children who have been baptized and are living as faithful disciples. Many feel that the children must remain faithful their whole life for a man to stay in the office of an elder. Others believe that the children must be respectful, but once they are adults, out of their parents' charge, their personal life should not affect an elder's qualification. The approach each church takes requires discussion and study as men are considered for appointment.

Another discussion concerning qualifications of elders concerns whether or not the lists found in 1 Timothy 3, Titus 1, and 1 Peter 5 are qualifications for an elder or qualities of the type of man to be considered for the role. Are these guidelines for the totality of the character of the man considered, or are they lists of "in or out" qualifications? One problem with the "in or out" approach is that we can make one or two of the listed qualifications more important than the rest. Our fellowship of churches has put a great deal of emphasis on the children being disciples, yet not as much on being known for hospitality. There is a need for a balanced approach to the instructions of Peter and Paul as we look at the candidates for eldership.

Qualities of an Elder

The first quality Paul and Peter describe in their letters to Timothy and the churches undergoing persecution is to look for a man who desires to be an elder (1 Timothy 3:1) or is willing and eager to be an elder (1 Peter 5:2). Paul uses the phrase "Here is a trustworthy saying" to emphasize this important quality in any man appointed as an elder. A man is appointed as an elder because he eagerly and earnestly desires to love and serve the church as Christ loved her. Paul describes this as a "noble task." It is a noble task because Christ purchased the church with his own blood.

The knowledge and conviction that this is a noble task, a fine work, is a necessary quality for an elder—since he will face many problems and trials as he carries out the role of overseer and shepherd. It will take the sacrifice of his life in many ways, so this must be his full desire.

The Apostle Paul wrote to the churches in Ephesus and Crete concerning the type of man to appoint to the eldership. These two churches had different backgrounds and needs. Ephesus was a more mature church that had elders for several years. It had faced many attacks from divisive false teachers and from the pagan world of Ephesus. Was there a need to replace older elders or just appoint new ones as the church grew? The Scriptures do not make this clear.

Crete was an island of many small settlements, and Paul had left Titus to complete what he was not able to finish. We do not know if they were merely younger churches without elders or if in Crete it was taking a long time to get men spiritually ready to be elders. Peter was addressing a scattered church that was undergoing severe persecution. Each list of qualities addressed the needs of the church in its particular situation.

The Scriptures teach that the qualifications of an elder fall into three general categories of character: public and spiritual life, family life, and private life.

Public and Spiritual Life

If we combine the qualifications of a man's public and spiritual life, we learn that an elder is to be:

- Respectable (1 Timothy 3:2)
- Above reproach (1 Timothy 3:2)
- Blameless (Titus 1:6–7)
- Reputable with outsiders (1 Timothy 3:7)
- Honest, not pursuing dishonest gain (Titus 1:7)
- Hospitable (1 Timothy 3:2, Titus 1:8)

- Not given to drunkenness (1 Timothy 3:3)
- Not violent but gentle (1 Timothy 3:3)
- Not quarrelsome (1 Timothy 3:3)
- Not overbearing (Titus 1:7, 1 Peter 5:3: not lording it over)
- Not quick-tempered (Titus 1:7)
- Not a recent convert (1 Timothy 3:6)
- Holding firmly to the trustworthy message as it had been taught (Titus 1:9)
- Able to teach (1 Timothy 3:2)

He is to be respected in and out of the church in such a way that no one would be able to fault his character. An elder must be able to relate to people using gentleness and patience. In times of distress, personal and church difficulties, or persecution, the church needs men with these qualities.

An elder must know the word of God and be able to teach the truth to the disciples. There will be attacks from Satan against the message, coming through false teaching from within and without the church. An elder is to provide protection for the disciples from such attacks.

Family Life

Since the Bible recognizes that a man must first be able to manage his family well before he is considered for managing the affairs of the church, we should understand what the Scriptures teach about his family life. We see several qualities of family life. An elder must:

- Be the husband of one wife (1 Timothy 3:2; Titus 1:6)
- Have children who believe (Titus 1:6)
- Not have children who are open to the charge of being wild and disobedient (Titus 1:6)
- Have children who obey him (1 Timothy 3:4)

- Manage his own family well in a manner worthy of full respect (1 Timothy 3:4)

What does it mean to be the "husband of one wife?" The Greek says that an elder is to be a "one-woman man," but the meaning is not completely clear when translated. Situations where a man has divorced before becoming a Christian and then remarried, or a spouse has died and the man remarries are becoming more and more frequent as the church reaches out to the world and our membership ages. Each congregation will need to decide how they handle these questions as men are considered for the eldership.

If we look at the qualities described for the wife of a deacon and apply those same qualities to the wife of an elder, we will see several attributes mentioned. (The Scriptures use the term "the women" in 1 Timothy 3:11. There are differing thoughts among scholars as to whether this refers to women deacons [deaconesses], wives of deacons, or wives of elders. Either way, the qualities mentioned would be applicable for respected women.) The women are to be:

- Worthy of respect (1 Timothy 3:11)
- Not malicious talkers (1 Timothy 3:11)
- Temperate (1 Timothy 3:11)
- Trustworthy in everything (1 Timothy 3:11)

As previously discussed, often the behavior of the candidate's children is the first qualification examined. Many books and studies have been written on this subject with a variety of interpretations. This topic should be discussed and studied thoroughly when considering a man for the eldership.

Private Life

The integrity of a man's character is measured by what he does in private, when no one is looking. An elder must be:

- Self-controlled (Titus 1:8)
- Upright (Titus 1:8)
- Holy (Titus 1:8)
- Disciplined (Titus 1:8)
- Temperate (1 Timothy 3:3)
- Not a lover of money or pursuing dishonest gain (1 Timothy 3:3; 1 Peter 5:2)

These are qualities that describe the character of a man and should be known by those closest to him. A man's private life shows who he is before God and reflects his inner desires. Certainly, openness about such things as sexual purity, financial management, addictions of any kind, anger, and uplifting and pure speech are vital for one who desires the role of an elder.

Conclusion

The man who is selected as an elder is one who is willing and prepared to accept the roles of overseer and shepherd of the body of Christ. He has shown himself able to lead his family well, to earn the respect of disciples and non-Christians, and to have self-control over his life as he walks with God in love and truth. No one is perfect, but Paul and Peter give us the picture of the man that could become a part of the eldership. Elders have the noble task of guiding, directing, and protecting the disciples. The men selected are to be of the highest personal and public character as they continue to grow into the likeness of Christ.

40

Chapter Five

The Heart of a Shepherd

Bill Hooper and Dan Liu

The Old and New Testaments are filled with references to shepherds. At times these verses refer directly to someone who looks after a flock of sheep or herd of goats, while in other instances the Scriptures describe a shepherd as one responsible for looking after God's flock, God's people. Many of these verses refer directly to God himself as the Shepherd.

We will begin by looking at examples from the Scriptures so as to better understand what God wants to tell us about a shepherd's heart. In the first part of this chapter we will survey several instances of the word "shepherd" in the Bible. In the second part we will offer our thoughts on what we believe a shepherd is called to *do*, and what a shepherd is called to *be* for God's kingdom today.

God as a Shepherd

David put it simply in Psalm 23 when he said, "The Lord is my shepherd." Isaiah described the Sovereign Lord in this way:

> He tends his flock like a shepherd:
> > He gathers the lambs in his arms
> > and carries them close to his heart;
> > > he gently leads those that have young (Isaiah 40:11)

This helps us understand why God would proclaim, "You are my sheep, the sheep of my pasture, and I am your God, declares the Sovereign Lord" (Ezekiel 34:31).

Prophets, Priests and Kings as Shepherds

God envisioned his prophets, priests and kings as strong and loving shepherds who would take great care of his people. For example, through Samuel God called for David while he was tending the sheep in the field, to anoint him as Israel's king. In 1 Samuel 17 we read of David's character and courage as he cared for his father's sheep. The Bible refers to David as "a man after [God's] own heart" (1 Samuel 13:14; Acts 13:22). As Asaph writes,

> He chose David his servant
>   and took him from the sheep pens;
> from tending the sheep he brought him
>   to be the shepherd of his people Jacob,
>   of Israel his inheritance.
> And David shepherded them with integrity of heart;
>   with skillful hands he led them. (Psalm 78:70–72)

God also expected the priests and prophets of Israel to shepherd his people well, but they often failed miserably at the task. God spoke through Jeremiah to bemoan the condition of his people and rebuke the shepherds for misleading the flock.

> "My people have been lost sheep;
>   their shepherds have led them astray
>   and caused them to roam on the mountains.
> They wandered over mountain and hill
>   and forgot their own resting place." (Jeremiah 50:6)

The Lord again rebuked Israel's shepherds in Ezekiel 34:2–3.

> "Son of man, prophesy against the shepherds of Israel; prophesy and say to them: 'This is what the Sovereign LORD says: "Woe to you shepherds of Israel who only take care of yourselves! Should not shepherds take care of the flock? You eat the curds, clothe yourselves with the wool and slaughter the choice animals, but you do not take care of the flock."'"

God deplored the selfishness of these shepherds and lambasted them with a litany of their failings.

> "You have not strengthened the weak or healed the sick or bound up the injured. You have not brought back the strays or searched for the lost. You have ruled over them harshly and brutally. So they were scattered because there was no shepherd, and when they were scattered they became food for all the wild animals." (Ezekiel 34:4–5)

The Old Testament reminds us time and again about God's expectations for the heart of a shepherd. His prophets challenged Israel's shepherds in their selfishness, and yet the Scriptures also give us a glimpse into an example of a shepherd's selflessness in David. Throughout this earlier testament, in the not-too-distant background, God's own example looms powerfully as the ultimate Shepherd.

Jesus as a Shepherd

In the New Testament God clearly displays the example of the heart of a shepherd in his own Son, Jesus. John 10:3–16 shows Jesus' love and heart for his sheep. He describes the essence of spiritual leadership—the sheep follow the shepherd because they know and trust him, and the shepherd calls each sheep by name. He leads, protects, cares for, and loves his sheep. The Good Shepherd willingly lays down his life for them. A hired hand tends sheep for money and abandons them when danger arises, but the Good Shepherd stands by to protect them. Jesus looked out upon the crowds and "had compassion on them, because they were harassed and helpless, like sheep without a shepherd" (Matthew 9:36). As Jesus taught in the Parable of the Lost Sheep (Luke 15:1–7), a good shepherd will go after the one lost sheep, rejoicing when it is found. Another New Testament writer simply referred to Jesus as "that great Shepherd of the sheep" (Hebrews 13:20).

The Apostles' Example & Teaching on Being a Shepherd

Just as Jesus taught and modeled shepherd leadership, he called specifically on the apostle Peter to follow his example. After his resurrection, Jesus charged Peter three times to feed and take care of his sheep (John 21:15–19). We see later in Peter's teaching that he reflected this charge to others as he appealed to his fellow elders to love and care for God's church, following Christ's example.

> Be shepherds of God's flock that is under your care, watching over them—not because you must, but because you are willing, as God wants you to be; not pursuing dishonest gain, but eager to serve; not lording it over those entrusted to you, but being examples to the flock. And when the Chief Shepherd appears, you will receive the crown of glory that will never fade away. (1 Peter 5:2–4)

In another context, the Apostle Paul pleaded with the elders of Ephesus to keep watch over themselves and the entire flock that the Holy Spirit had placed under their shepherding, guarding the flock from savage wolves and serving responsibly and with integrity (Acts 20:28–32). Reminding them of the costliness of this charge, Paul called them to "be shepherds of the church of God, which he bought with his own blood" (Acts 20:28b).

Shepherds for Today

If we take a moment to contemplate all that these scriptures tell us about being a shepherd of God's people, we can see that the weight of responsibility is great. The culmination of the Old Testament testimony on the heart of a shepherd finds its fulfillment in the New Testament in Jesus' example and the teachings of the apostles. Following this image of a shepherd-leader, we are reminded of his courage and perseverance. God's word repeatedly reinforces to us a shepherd's selflessness and genuine care for each member of his flock. Throughout the Scriptures a shepherd of God's people is expected to have unconditional love for God's sheep, the body of Christ, his church.

Given these teachings, what should a shepherd after God's own heart do today as he oversees the flock? And what qualities would dominate this shepherd's heart?

What Elders Are Called to Do

From our earlier scriptural survey we recall that Ezekiel 34 reminds us of the high calling that God expects from his shepherds, both then and today. The passage gives us guidelines concerning unconditional love for the church—what it looks like and what shepherds (or elders) filled with the right heart would do. If we reverse the picture of the selfish shepherd to imagine what a selfless shepherd would do, we can envision him fulfilling the following list of responsibilities: you have strengthened the weak, healed the sick, bound up the injured, brought back the strays, searched for the lost, and ruled them gently and kindly.

Let's examine each one of these responsibilities more closely:

Strengthen the Weak

Discerning elders will know the condition of their flocks (Proverbs 27:23). The weak in any flock need more care. They may find it harder to feed themselves, so attention to their nurturing in God's word is critical. The elder who strengthens the weak will do so consistently and patiently, in one-on-one sessions with them, in small groups of disciples, and when he preaches and teaches in public. As Paul admonished those in Ephesus, "By this kind of hard work we must help the weak, remembering the words the Lord Jesus himself said: 'It is more blessed to give than to receive'" (Acts 20:35).

Heal the Sick

Faithful prayer means a great deal to disciples and to God, so an elder must make himself available to those in need of it. Even in fellowship, when disciples ask us to pray for them we can stop at that moment and do so. James 5:14 says: "Is anyone among you sick? Let them call the elders of the church to pray over them and anoint them with oil in the name of the Lord." This passage also addresses the spiritual healing that can occur. In all things, "the prayer of a righteous person is powerful and effective" (verse 16).

Bind Up the Injured

An injured disciple has had his faith hurt or damaged. For example, the loss of a loved one can challenge even the very strong among us.

During these times it is not what is said so much as just being present that can make a difference.

Bring Back the Strays

Over the years, we have had far too many of those whom we have baptized leave our fellowship—and we still do. Restoring those who have left requires great care and can take a long time to accomplish. Elders play a great role in bringing back the strays. They also help prevent loss from the flock by strengthening the weak.

Search for the Lost

Like all Christians, we who are also called to be elders are commissioned to make disciples of all nations, to seek and save the lost. The mission given to us by God must always be exemplified in our personal lives.

Kindly and Gently Lead

In Ezekiel 34 the prophet calls out those selfish shepherds for ruling with force, severity, and harshness. Elders with a shepherd's heart will be servant leaders. They will lead with strength, but also with love, firm in the truth but affirming the weak and those in need of encouragement. Perhaps more than anything, the example an elder provides to the flock leads them more powerfully than any other aspect of his life.

What Elders Are Called to Be

The list of tasks above provides guidance to what an elder can do, but in the end, whatever an elder does only reflects who he is as a man, before others and before God. And who he is as a man is reflected by what is in his heart.

> Above all else, guard your heart,
> for everything you do flows from it. (Proverbs 4:23)

We can be fully assured that God has provided ample instruction as to what the heart of a shepherd should look like. Based on our survey of the Scriptures and what elders are called to do, in this final section we will examine what we believe elders are called to be—what the heart of a shepherd should look like.

A Heart in Love with God

Nothing speaks more loudly, whether to hundreds or to the one, than one's personal walk with God. The shepherd's heart should be like that of David, who expressed repeatedly in the Psalms his deep gratitude for simply having a personal relationship with his Lord. David must have cultivated this intimacy with God during his early years as he watched over his sheep—praying, singing, writing music, and meditating before the Lord. Such a relationship empowered him to face later challenges against Goliath, Saul, and others. A shepherd after God's heart tells him his inmost secrets and finds complete security in him. How does my walk with God compare to David's? Would God say that I am a man after his own heart?

Full of Integrity and Honesty

Remember that every word is valued and measured. We recall that David was known for shepherding the people with "integrity of heart." Regarding the handling of funds, Paul reminded the Corinthians of the importance of doing what is right before both God and man (2 Corinthians 8:21). Even his enemies noted that Jesus was a man of integrity (Matthew 22:16). An elder after God's heart should have the reputation of being a man of integrity and honesty, a man of steel and velvet. He should say what he means and mean what he says. Being both loving and strong in character means he will stand up and speak the truth in love with wisdom from God's word. For the elder whose heart is full of integrity and honesty, there will be times that difficult decisions must be made. Such times call for much prayer and fasting, deep convictions, and a close walk with God.

A Heart of Humility and Strength

In 1 Peter 5:5–6, Peter exhorts us, "Clothe yourselves with humility toward one another, because, 'God opposes the proud but shows favor to the humble.' Humble yourselves, therefore, under God's mighty hand, that he may life you up in due time." He also instructs in verse 3 to shepherd by "not lording it over those entrusted to you, but being examples to the flock."

Pray for wisdom, humility, and guidance from God's Holy Spirit. Seek wisdom, humility, and guidance from brothers and sisters around you. As Paul admonishes us in Philippians 2:3–4, "Do nothing out of selfish ambition or vain conceit. Rather, in humility value others above yourselves, not looking to your own interests but each of you to the interests of the others."

Living as a shepherd requires great humility—in exercising judgment in difficult matters, understanding differing perspectives, and even in balancing the demands of time and energy from church and family.

In his book *They Smell Like Sheep,* Dr. Lynn Anderson writes,

> Today's spiritual shepherds must be able to put criticism in proper perspective. They must be good listeners on one hand and clear thinkers on the other. Above all, they must be able to absorb hostility over the long haul, becoming neither hardened and insensitive nor bitter, angry, or defensive. The challenge demands great strength of character and the emotional health that flows out of peace with God.[2]

In his book *Dynamic Leadership,* Gordon Ferguson makes the following statement:

> Humility, properly understood, does not reduce confidence—it increases it. Why? If we are prideful, we are depending upon our own strength; if we are humble, we are depending upon God's strength.[3]

The heart of a shepherd is eager to learn and to imitate. If you are asked to be a part of a shepherds-in-training group, open up your life in humility and openness, and eagerly learn everything you can. Share

---

[2] Dr. Lynn Anderson, *They Smell Like Sheep* (West Monroe, LA: Howard Publishing, 1997), 182.

[3] Gordon Ferguson, *Dynamic Leadership* (Spring, TX: Illumination Publishers, 2012), 184.

every corner of your life no matter how dark it seems. Our lives should be an open book. Trust God with your life, because he cares for you.

Full of Love and Compassion

Keep those home fires burning. After God, your wife comes first and your children next. The example you set with your marriage and family leads the way in demonstrating the qualities of a shepherd. You must love your wife, present her as a radiant bride before Christ, and shepherd your family with conviction and with love. How can you manage the household of God if you cannot manage your own family well? (1 Timothy 3:4).

Open your homes and show the love and compassion that flows from a redeemed life. Reach out to all in the church family, those who are weak as well as the strong. Touch people's lives physically, emotionally, socially, and spiritually. Elders are not first appointed and then start shepherding. They are recognized for their shepherding heart and example, one that has been displayed for years. If we are wise, we will seek out the more mature among us who can share their experiences—the successes and failures, the good and the bad—so that we do not try to "reinvent the wheel" or feel alone. From all this, we can know what to do and what qualities to demonstrate in our lives. Let's follow the teaching, learn from the wise, and ultimately, put our faith in God so that others may see in our lives the heart of a shepherd.

50

Chapter Six

COMPANIONS IN LEADERSHIP: WISDOM FROM OUR WIVES

Note from the editors: No man would be qualified to become an elder without his wife. We believe our wives are a vital part of our role. Their spiritual insight, wisdom, and integrity strengthens us and completes us. They are not appendages, but united with us heart and soul as they, too, minister to the church. None of us could fulfill this role without the sacrifice and wisdom of our wives—their current contributions and their legacies.

In this section our wives each share one aspect of being an elder's wife that they wish to pass on to others who are currently wives of elders, or whose husbands are considering becoming an elder. As you read these contributions you will better understand why we so deeply value our wives. Don't skip over these valuable insights, brothers. Remember, we are in this together.

Accepting the Call
Sharon Gauthier – Chicago, Illinois

The term "elder's wife" or "deacon's wife" can kindle thoughts of insecurity in many of us. We may even think, "My husband is a great man of God, but I'm only in this role because I'm married to him." This self-doubting internal dialogue sabotages the great work God plans to do through us.

When my husband and I were asked to go into the ministry years ago, I remember thinking, "But I have so many flaws! Do they know how fearful I can be to share my faith? Do they know how disrespectful

I can be toward my husband? Do they know that sometimes I miss my daily quiet times?" I doubted my ability and God's call for me.

After I opened up to a sister about my struggle, she showed me a scripture that completely changed my thinking—Exodus 3. As God called Moses, he made it clear that the call was not about Moses at all! God called Moses because he heard the cry of his people. Likewise, when God calls me, it is not because I am so amazing. Instead, it is because of the cry of people seeking God. For whatever reason, God uses imperfect people to fulfill his perfect mission.

If you are struggling with the call to be an "elder's wife," "deacon's wife," or simply a woman who helps other women spiritually—keep in mind that the call is not about you. God knows your weaknesses, just as he knew Moses'. If your husband has been asked to consider the eldership, it is not an accident that you are his wife. God knows who your husband is married to. Remember God's words to Moses in Exodus 3:12, "I will be with you." God is perfectly capable of doing his work. All he asks is that we put our full trust in him and answer the call.

Learn While You Listen

Erlyn Sugarman – Los Angeles, California

There was a time when I thought that I was a good communicator; after all, I could talk up a storm and fight to have the last word. That notion changed when I started reading the Bible and came across James 1:19, "Everyone should be quick to listen [and] slow to speak."

Communication is not all about speaking, it is much more about listening. I learned this valuable lesson through an interaction with a friend from church. Every Sunday when I would see her I would ask her how she and her kids were doing. Her constant reply would be, "Oh we're hanging in there." At one midweek service, something prompted me to ask her what she had done over the weekend. Surprisingly, her face lit up as she recounted the wonderful day she spent with her kids. They hiked, talked, laughed, and had a picnic at the beach. The next day she called me to thank me for asking and listening.

I am amazed at how much I learn when I listen to others. I hear their pain, grief, loneliness, and needs. I also hear their joys, victories, and dreams. I even hear their talents. It is a known fact that women talk more than men. We can speak, but we must also listen. Women are extraordinary—we can multitask.

Listening is powerful. We can connect mind to mind, see eye to eye, and through hearing each other we are able to "get" one another. When I listen to someone I can connect heart to heart. I feel what they feel; I understand them and relate to what they are going through. That's when I see the whole picture, connect the dots, and can take action.

There's someone we must always choose to listen to. In the book of 1 Kings 19:11–12 God said,

> "Go out, and stand on the mountain before the LORD." And behold, the LORD passed by, and a great and strong wind tore into the mountains and broke the rocks in pieces before the LORD, but the LORD was not in the wind; and after the wind an earthquake, but the LORD was not in the earthquake; and after the earthquake a fire, but the LORD was not in the fire; and after the fire a still small voice. (NKJV)

It may be a still small voice, but it is a persistent voice. The Spirit speaks to us to guide us, direct, and lead us. When we listen to the Holy Spirit, we hear the heart of God.

His Grace Is Sufficient
Erica Kim – Denver, Colorado

> Three times I pleaded with the Lord to take it away from me. But he said to me, "My grace is sufficient for you, for my power is made perfect in weakness." Therefore I will boast all the more gladly about my weaknesses, so that Christ's power may rest on me. (2 Corinthians 12:8–9)

If you could wave a magic wand, what would you want Jesus to take away from you? Maybe it's your financial burdens, your sickness, your spouse's illness, your temptations, your relationship conflicts, your child's struggles, or your work pressures.

Since the age of twenty-five, I have fought a disease called SLE (Systemic Lupus Erythematosus). During the ensuing years I have felt like an eighty-five-year-old in my twenties, thirties, and forties, and now into my fifties. I cannot say that I have ever felt energetic, strong, or full of health for most of my life. I almost died at the age of twenty-six from this disease, but through the prayers of many and the treatment of great doctors I was able to experience a short seven years of remission in my thirties, during which time I was able to serve in God's kingdom more actively.

Jesus says in the passage above, "My power is made perfect in weakness." For many years I could not understand what that truly meant. How could his power be made "perfect" in weakness? Power is supposed to be strength, vitality, and energy. I had none of those. Moreover, I had gotten really stuck on that one word: perfect.

Even Jesus was tempted to ask God to save him from his hour of suffering and death. Jesus lived, suffered, and died so that God could be glorified (John 12:23–24). It was at the time of the crucifixion, at Christ's weakest time and perhaps his greatest temptation, God's power and glory shone the brightest. God's power is made perfect in weakness—even in the weakness of Jesus!

As I look back on my life, I see his grace and how God's plan for me is perfect. In fact, my illness allows me to cherish the moments I have with my family and to have deeper compassion for others who suffer chronically. It teaches me to be a better wife, ministry leader, mother, and friend. Most of all, it molds me into being more like Christ.

If I had a magic wand today and not twenty-five years ago, I would choose to live with my illness again. I see that his grace is truly sufficient for me. I would not be the person I am today without it. Now every day is a gift I treasure.

In the same way, whatever you might want to have "disappear" from your life today might be essential for you to live a life of grace in Christ. It may be the greatest blessing in disguise!

Initiate Initiative

Jeanie Shaw – Boston, Massachusetts

Women of faith throughout the Bible often did not know what to do when faced with challenging situations. Consider Abigail and Esther, who didn't know exactly what to do in tough circumstances—but prayed and did something. They initiated, not knowing how their actions would be received. Consider Miriam, whose pure gratitude and awe of God caused her to lead the Israelite women in song and praise, inspiring great faith. These women (and many more) stepped out of their comfort zones and onto their faith. They took initiative.

I have at times hesitated in fear and at other times stepped out in faith. The latter is a better choice! When I was pregnant with our first child, I wished to take an exercise class for pregnant women. No gyms offered such a class, so I asked a neighborhood gym if they would pay me to teach one. Surprisingly, they did. Garbed in a purple sweat suit (and looking like an Easter egg), I took my Jane Fonda VHS exercise tape and took (taught) my prenatal exercise class while getting paid to do so. Had I failed to initiate with the gym owner, I would have missed this opportunity. While that class was of no spiritual significance, this silly example reminds me of the value of initiative. More often than we think, our initiative (or lack thereof) can reap eternal consequences.

We can often see obstacles and fail to respond. Women have a unique vantage point to see various needs and weaknesses—with the women, within the church, within the leadership, with the youth, and in myriad relational dynamics. We can either sit back with a critical eye or step forward with solutions—turning to God for wisdom, and then working together as a community, "rallying the troops" to offer their gifts toward meeting the need.

Perhaps we feel like we still aren't old enough, wise enough, or qualified enough—or that someone else can do it better. Perhaps we are afraid we will mess something up or will receive a negative response. Remember, God will be with us in our faith, as he was with Abigail, Esther, and Miriam.

Sisters, if your husband is becoming (or is) an elder, part of the reason is because he has a spiritual wife—you! Our years of reading the Bible, watching God work, and experiencing victories and failures help us be those mature teachers spoken of in Hebrews 5:14: "But solid food is for the mature, who by constant use have trained themselves to distinguish good from evil."

Like it or not, we are the "older women" whom God calls to teach and train others—to take initiative (Titus 2:3–4). If we don't, who will?

May we have the faith to pray—and then step out boldly.

Peaceful, Purposeful Home
Sally Hooper – Dallas, Texas

As Bill's favorite partner in the gospel and his wife, I take my role very seriously. God did not make me an elder, but the wife of an elder—and along with that privilege I have many responsibilities and areas where I can make a difference in his effectiveness in the way he serves.

A peaceful home: Proverbs 31:12 tells us, "She brings him good, not harm, all the days of her life." When I asked Bill what was the most helpful quality I add to him as an elder's wife, he shared how he valued having our home as a place where he can think about the issues at hand without being surrounded by clutter and chaos. Bill helps tremendously with household responsibilities, but it is always on my mind to make sure that our home is neat and orderly. Unfortunately, that has not always been the case, and I have learned (and am learning) to put away my stacks and piles of papers and other items into their proper places.

I have also learned that timing is everything when I have issues to discuss with him. When he is hungry, tired, or has just arrived home from a trying meeting, it is not the time to start an intense conversation. Peaceful resolutions come when the timing is right and we treat each other considerately. Husbands and wives will grow as they practice "timeliness" with each other.

A useful home: 1 Peter 1:13 says, "Therefore, prepare your minds for action" (NASB). I must be mentally prepared so that our home is ready for "action!" God gave us our home, and he expects us to use it for him. When we bought our home more than twenty years ago, we prayed over it and asked God to allow us to always use it for him. Since then, hundreds of people have come into our home for dinner, meetings, studies, classes, and friendship times. There are occasions when we meet others out at a restaurant, but it never takes the place of having them into our home. When they leave our home they may not remember what they ate, but prayerfully they will always remember how special they felt.

God Is the "Fixer"
Gloria Baird – formerly Phoenix, now Paradise

One of the biggest blessings of my life is being Al Baird's wife! Another blessing that has come with that role is becoming the wife of an elder in God's church. I love being an elder's wife. While it is an incredible privilege, it is also a daunting challenge. I knew that it was a big responsibility, and early on I wasn't sure I was equipped for the task.

I could see Al's qualifications, but my insecurities about myself loomed large in my eyes. Of course, looking back over the years I see God's hand in molding, shaping, and teaching us so much from one experience to the next.

Working with God's people means dealing with a lot of varied situations and problems. Just about the time we thought we had seen or heard of everything, a brand-new set of circumstances would present itself—and come to us for solutions and help. I had thought that meant we were expected to have the answers. That put added pressure on us, because others expected us to have the answers too. There were certainly times when I felt inadequate, or even a failure in helping people change.

A huge life lesson for me was realizing that I can't repent or change for someone else; each person is responsible for his or her own actions, thoughts, and feelings. I had earlier thought that we were to "fix" someone, and when that didn't happen I would go on a "downer," feeling like we had failed. After experiencing this more times than I would like to admit, it finally connected with me that I cannot fix anyone. GOD is the Fixer!

What an amazing load that truth took off my shoulders! It has been so helpful for me as we continue to do all we can do to be with people as they go through their own journeys. I continue to share this lesson with others as often as I can, so that our dependence is on God and not on ourselves. It is such a relief to know that God provides what we need just as we need it. It is all about God—and not about what we know and experience.

May we always look to God for our strength, help, and wisdom.

The Power of Truth
Linda Brumley – San Diego, California

Once while sincerely contemplating Ephesians 4:15, I had to confront my tendency to speak the truth harshly or in frustration. Hmmm…not like Jesus. I worked at reversing (aka, repenting of) this bent. This was hard to do. I had to be intentional and alert. It is still a conviction from which I can slip away.

I put my focus appropriately on the "in love" part. That involved my demeanor, my tone, and most of all my heart.

Some recent observations have made me aware that, while love is the greatest command, truth has its own spiritual power. Our Lord, after all, is truth (John 14:6). Truth—simple, unapologetic, often unpopular. It takes courage to speak truth.

I've seen wives in verbally abusive relationships grow in their confidence in the truth of who they are before God, and say to their husbands in heated situations, "I am a daughter of God and you should not talk to me that way." It was said firmly but quietly and had amazing results in terms of helping their husbands treat them differently.

I've seen mothers lovingly confront a deceitful child with truth, and even when the child walked away without owning up to their misdemeanor, they returned later to confess.

We live in a world more concerned with how things are said than with how true they are. God certainly advocates for gracious speech, and there is power in grace; but there is also great power in truth (Colossians 4:6). It should give us confidence that God uses truth to impact human hearts; when we speak truth we unleash the power of God. We can be sure we are speaking truth when we speak from the Bible.

A Titus 2 Tip
Pat Brush – South Florida

> Likewise, teach the older women to be reverent in the way they live…to teach what is good. Then they can train the younger women to love their husbands and children, to be self-controlled and pure, to be busy at home, to be kind, and to be subject to their husbands, so that no one will malign the word of God. (Titus 2:3–5)

"Sometimes it just doesn't seem worth it to come to church." The mother of the wailing baby started to cry. "I end up in a corner of the building so she won't disturb anyone; I don't get to sing, fellowship, or hear the sermon. I really feel alone. Why even come?"

I paused before responding. Did she want my opinion? Was she looking for advice? Asking for help? I considered my comrades—middle-aged moms who'd endured colicky children, toted kids to multiple services on a Sunday, pew-wrestled toddlers in the pre-Kingdom Kids era…my recollection proved us to be virtual Worship Warriors.

My first thought was, *Toughen up.* What I said was, "Why not ask one of the older women what they did with their baby?"

"Oh, several have come up and said, 'You should try this.' I've gotten lots of advice. But I guess I just want someone to listen. I would love to feel like someone is going through it with me."

This was surprising. Increasingly, it seemed to me that younger women didn't want anything from older women.

Older woman: I could help with the question you are Googling right now. Just ask me.

Younger woman: Uh huh.

As I age, I wonder how much longer my life experience will be relevant. I try to stay informed. Reading a "Trending Now" post helps me feel, well…trendy. But I want my life to count, to make a difference, to be a kind of opener-of-doors to younger women as they follow Jesus in a culture and climate that can feel like Mars to me.

And that is why Titus 2 tells older women to "teach what is good." I may prefer to dispense advice like a pharmacist, but the master Teacher met people and walked alongside them. What Jesus taught was good. And it was needed. Relationships are messy. They take time and lots of work. I can think that at my age I've earned the right for it to be easier, for the younger to come to me for sage insights and "back in my day" stories. But I know that there are times when they don't know what they don't know. So, "what is good" is to walk with them: to initiate with the younger women, to open my home for get-togethers, to ask for and listen to their ideas, to pose the curious questions and genuinely desire to understand their answers. I am finding that my experiences, my stories, and my deeply held beliefs are meaningful to them. Like me, they are passionate about making life changes "so that no one will malign the word of God."

In truth, I am learning about "what is good" from younger women. In the times we share together, whether it is a Bible study, a ministry staff meeting, or a social interaction, my young friends tend to be more generous in their characterization of others, use more discretion and sensitivity in conversations, and strive for sincerity without spin. The younger women are helping me be more "reverent in the way [I] live."

And so, I am learning to take to heart the cry of that young mother who, in loneliness and uncertainty, needs friendship and a listening ear. My first instinct may be to "fix it." But I pray and ask the Teacher to help me keep in step beside her.

Short Talks with Long Effects
Geri Laing – Myrtle Beach, South Carolina

I still remember, as a young college student and new Christian, how much I was impacted by the older women in the church. Some of them I got to know more intimately outside of church activities, but many of them I felt a bond with simply because of short but meaningful interactions in the fellowship. They made me feel that I was cared about, noticed, remembered—and that I was a valued part of my new family.

Sisters, we have no idea the power we have as women to create a sense of warmth, love, and family in our churches. And much of it is done not by scheduling more appointments, but by our loving presence during the fellowship times before and after our services. It may be just a warm greeting, a smile, a hug, a short conversation, an encouraging word, or even something as simple as remembering a person's name. I cannot overstate the difference that these seemingly insignificant gestures of love and concern make. Not only do they give others a sense of being loved and of belonging, but when a younger Christian or a younger person sees older disciples still loving, caring, and smiling after years of serving God, they are inspired and their own faith is strengthened. They believe that they, too, can make it.

I am encouraged by Jesus' example. Notice how many short conversations Jesus had (in passing) that changed lives. We often become overwhelmed because we truthfully don't have any more times in our schedules for actual meetings, dinners, or appointments. But we do have time for short yet meaningful exchanges in the fellowship! It means that we have to be mindful, present, and fully engaged when we are among our sisters and brothers. Then they will want to have the same spirit of love and concern that they see in us. It is contagious, and it creates family!

> Be very careful then, how you live—not as unwise but as wise, making the most of every opportunity, because the days are evil. (Ephesians 5:15–16)

I believe that times we spend together in the fellowship are some of the most valuable in our churches for us as elders' wives. We need to make the most of these few hours in the week when the disciples are together. Love them, touch them, notice them, ask them meaningful questions. Help them feel that they are part of a warm and loving family. I deeply believe that our times together as a church, just as with our own families, are invaluable moments of renewal and refreshment before we go back out into a dark and fallen world.

Not all of us will be powerful speakers and Bible teachers, but all of us as mature Christian women have the ability to love our brothers and sisters with our smiles, hugs, words of wisdom, and encouragement. Next time you meet as the family of God, I urge you—give your whole self and love with all your heart!

> "By this will everyone know that you are my disciples, if you love one another." (John 13:35)

Work Out Your Own Salvation with Vulnerability

Elexa Liu – Hong Kong, China

I have met many amazing elders' wives in my years as a Christian. Each one has impressed me with her unique qualities. One of them is a no-nonsense person. Another is gentle in spirit. Still another is generous and unselfish.

There are many others, but they are all unbelievably spiritual.

I have often wondered if I really "qualify" as an elder's wife. After all, I am here by default, am I not?

The truth is, I struggle with feeling competent, both at my job and in my role in the church. I am naturally judgmental and selfish. I feel envious of others more often than I like to admit.

God has blessed us with an apartment that is spacious by Hong Kong standards. For the past few months one of the campus Bible Talks started using our home for their outreach Bible discussions. I started out feeling fine about it. After all, this is God's house, not ours, right?

But after a few months, after some things got broken, dishes weren't put back in their place, or cleanup wasn't done accordingly, I started to have attitudes.

"Can I *not* have twenty young people at my house at 11 o'clock?" (i.e., I don't want to be giving).

"Shouldn't you guys have campus Bible Talk *on campus*?" (i.e., I don't want you using our house.)

"Can you guys make the Bible Talk smaller?" (i.e., this is too many people in this little apartment.)

I was NOT feeling too much like an elder's wife, at least not the ones I know.

I finally opened up to the two other elders' wives in the church, detailing all my struggles. We talked through my feelings and came up with practical steps I could take so I could continue to give, willingly and happily.

Would I have liked to not have any of those thoughts? Sure. Am I embarrassed that after being a Christian for over thirty years I still have this struggle? Yes! Do I still have the same selfish feelings? Sometimes.

But in order for me to make it to heaven (as an "elder's wife" or simply "Jane Christian"), I must be open; I must be authentic. It is only when I am real that I can truly work out my salvation—with fear and much trembling. Vulnerability does not come easy in my culture, and perhaps in any culture. We don't like to mess up. Yet when I am open with my struggles I can then "work out my salvation."

> Therefore, my dear friends,…continue to work out your salvation with fear and trembling. (Philippians 2:12)

When We Have Different Gift Sets
Kim Evans – Philadelphia, Pennsylvania

We all have traditions, habits, and cultures to which we are accustomed. Our churches today are comfortable with leadership scenarios where a husband and wife work together. Priscilla and Aquila serve as an example, and I do believe this is the simplest approach to ministry and eldership. It is a safe and direct approach. The challenge comes when we are called in different directions.

Before John the Baptist was born, Gabriel approached Zechariah to give him the news of a son, but when Jesus was going to be born, the angel Gabriel first went to Mary to herald the news. (Thank goodness the angel then went to Joseph. I can't imagine Mary trying to explain to Joseph that she was pregnant by the Holy Spirit—and no, we can't be together until after the baby is born. It would take an angel to help a husband understand this difficult truth.) In our churches we are more comfortable when the husband is called in a particular direction, but sometimes God calls the wife to a different area of leadership. In Proverbs

31, the noble wife considers a field and buys it out of her earnings. It doesn't seem that this is a team effort, but rather her husband has full confidence in her to conduct her business. She brings him good, not harm—but she is making some pretty big decisions on her own.

Shortly before Jesus' death he went to the home of Mary and Martha. It must have been a comforting place for him to visit, as he refers to the village as "the village of Mary and Martha." A single man goes to the home of two single women, and it is in the Scriptures—yikes. The example of the husband and wife team is powerful and is my favorite approach, but God sometimes works "out of the box."

God has called Walter and me in very different directions. Conflict resolution is a passion for Walter, and he is gifted in it. I have asked him if he would like me to take courses and grow in this area, but the truth is I am not very good at it. I am emotionally based, and the situations break my heart. He smiles at my request and says, "No, that's okay."

However, twenty-two years ago my heart was breaking because so many of the kids in our church were not wanting to become Christians. As I reflected back on my early days of being raised in the church, I remembered that I was at Michigan Christian Youth Camp when I first set my sights on being a Christian. I then realized that the kids in the church had nothing like what I had experienced as a child. My time at camp had a profound impact on molding me, so twenty-two years ago I dreamed of starting a camp for our kids in the church. Walter did not have the passion or the time to join this endeavor, but he supported me.

It's awkward at times to execute our dreams when God puts such things on a woman's heart. It is easier to have a dream and pass it off to a brother, but when God calls us to do something, we need to answer the call. Walter and I understand that God has given us very different callings and strengths. We support each other. It is clear that he is the elder and I am not, but God has chosen each of us to do what he has called us to do. I appreciate that my husband doesn't expect me to function in ways that are not the best use of my gift set, yet still supports me to accomplish what God put on my heart—helping the youth in church.

When each of us supports the other in the gifts God has given, we can become stronger together—and together help build up the kingdom of God.

Relationship with God
Mary Lou Craig – Boonton, New Jersey

One of the Lord's most precious promises to me is "Surely I am with you always, to the very end of the age" (Matthew 28:20). I have needed this assurance at every stage of life and in all of my roles—including that of elder's wife. My close relationship with God, shored up by daily Bible study, Scripture meditation, and prayer, is what keeps me going through thick and thin! As the Scriptures remind me day after day that God is the source of absolutely everything I need, I am able to persevere in loving and obeying him faithfully in my own life; and I am better able to help others find their way as well.

The wife described in Proverbs 31 fears the Lord. This relationship with God motivated her to live a life of noble character. She had wisdom and faithful instruction on her tongue. She brought her husband much good, not harm, throughout her life. And she could laugh at the days to come! All of these qualities are valuable in the role of an elder's wife. Our relationship with God helps us to be faithful, hopeful, and wise when we are called on to help in difficult situations. Our closeness to God and his word is a safeguard against relying on our own opinions or being swayed by society's strong pulls. We bring our husbands much good when we live out and teach other women the sound doctrine of the Bible. Our imperfect but ever-growing strength, faithfulness, and peace that come from a close walk with God can be such a source of inspiration and hope to those coming after us, including our own children. Thanks be to God for his powerful, amazing promise to be with us always!

It sounds simple and basic, but this promise (accompanied by our effort to draw near to him) is the only thing that will carry us through the joys and challenges that we face as leaders in the church of our Lord.

Chapter Seven

Shared Leadership: Elders and Other Gifted Roles

Frank Kim

Throughout history, from the building of edifices to the building of nations, even the most dynamic and gifted leaders would have been ineffective without the collective talents of others. Whether in sports, business, or societal change, the results of teamwork are unquestionable. In fact, the greater the goal, the stronger the team required to realize it.

Shared Leadership Is of God

The power of teamwork makes sense, since even the concept of relationships originally derives from the very nature of God and the example of Christ. In the creation account, God refers to himself as a plurality: "Let us make mankind in our image." In creating humans in his image, he created both man and woman. His vision for mankind was a great one—to fill and subdue the earth—and it would require a team.

Christ's vision was equally great and eternally important—to make saved disciples of all nations. To that end, he spent his few years of earthly ministry focused on developing a team. As history would eventually prove, Jesus' team was extraordinary, and as a shared leadership they experienced miraculous impact.

As elders of God's church, our desire to have God's heart and imitate Christ compels us to embrace the concept of shared leadership. God's vision and hope for his people are far too great for any individual to accomplish, no matter how spiritual or gifted he or she may be.

Shared Church Leadership Is Essential to Maturity

Just as an individual needs a team, an effective church leadership requires the balanced strengths of various roles. Ephesians 4:1–16 provides a concise, clear, and inspiring vision of shared leadership in the church, whether a local congregation or the global fellowship. Paul writes that Christ himself provided the various roles that comprise church leadership, specifically including those of evangelists, pastors (elders), and teachers (v11). These roles are each distinct in nature, yet completely align around the goal of maturing a church (vv12–16). The humble heart required to make such a partnership work is described at the beginning of the passage (vv1–6).

Perhaps the most inspiring aspect of this passage is what happens when a church truly has a shared leadership:

- We are equipped to serve (v12).
- We become unified in faith and knowledge of Christ (v13).
- We become mature, experiencing and reflecting the fullness of Christ (v13).
- We are protected from false teaching and temptation (v14).
- We have honest communication (v15).
- We hold up Jesus as head of the church (v15).
- We each experience playing a role in growing the body (v16).
- We experience love (v16).

Think about family. There are heroic single parents in our churches who do an amazing job raising their children, often with the caring support of other disciples. But can anyone deny that it greatly benefits a child to be raised by two loving parents who share the parenting responsibilities? In the same way, a church family that does not have an elder or evangelist or teacher can certainly grow and thrive. However, there is an extra depth of maturity reflected in the church when there is a balanced, shared leadership among our Christ-given roles.

The converse is also true: Immature leadership limits a church. Just as an unhealthy marriage affects the children, if a church leadership is immature in its relational dynamics, the church will feel the negative impact over time. With so much at stake, elders must be absolutely committed to a healthy shared leadership.

Differences Are Good: Elders, Evangelists, & Teachers

The leadership roles ordained by God—elders, evangelists, and teachers—certainly overlap in many areas, but they are also unique. By design, each role thinks differently, views the church differently, and brings unique gifts to our church's leadership. Those differences are healthy and essential to a maturing church.

In 2011, Wyndham Shaw, an elder of the Boston church, gave insightful descriptions of these primary roles in a lesson taught at the Western United States Elders' Conference in Estes Park, Colorado. I will attempt to summarize his remarks:[4]

Evangelists:
- spearhead the evangelistic mission of the church via setting priorities and personal example
- teach and preach with a prophetic edge
- train and hold other evangelists accountable
- have the leadership gift of administration and organization
- execute plans

Elders:
- spearhead shepherding and oversight of the church community's health
  - Evaluate by asking: "What's the atmosphere in the church? Is it healthy?"
- oversee the church: are responsible for OUTCOMES – functions can be delegated, but not the responsibility.
  - Ask "Where do we want to go, and are our leaders taking us there?"
  - Ask "Is our teaching making us healthy?"
- provide conflict resolution that maintains unity
- provide discipline that gives security to the church
- appoint leadership to meet needs of the church, including hiring senior staff and raising up new elders

---

[4] Wyndham Shaw, "God's Appointed Leaders," (Estes park, CO: Western US Elders Retreat, 2011).

Teachers:
- uphold the honor of God's word
- ground the church in the word
- create a systematic process to teach the Bible to leaders and members
- raise up other teachers

Obviously, in practice these roles can be far more complex and often intersect each other. However, as stated before, the differences are real and they are important. We must see these differences as complementary, not contradictory. Unfortunately, Satan will try to exploit contrasting perspectives to sow disunity within a church's leadership team. Maintaining unity requires an absolute commitment to communication, humility, and trust. On a shared leadership team, we must do more than simply hear one another. We must value, respect, and admire one another's perspectives and strengths. The cross-pollination of our views will lead to a deeper understanding of our church's health and will create a balanced vision of how to mature our ministry.

Evangelists Are Sheep Too

Elders can sometimes overlook the fact that full-time ministers are also members of the flock under their care. In other words, our ministers need our support, protection, guidance, and love. Too often, evangelists, women's ministry leaders, and teachers experience burnout from overwork or criticism. Their marriages and families can suffer from the lack of healthy boundaries between their personal lives and the never-ending needs of their ministry. In a truly shared leadership, elders must look after the other members of the leadership team and care for their spiritual, emotional, and physical well-being.

Elders can be best friends and confidantes to those in full-time ministry, serving as safe places for them to open up about their stresses, challenges, temptations, and sins. Elders can help members of the church to have reasonable, sustainable expectations of the ministry staff by clarifying publicly and privately that ministers need personal boundaries. Sometimes this may involve being a buffer to protect ministry staff from church members with unreasonable demands. Other times, it might be necessary to lovingly challenge a driven minister to spend more time connecting with his or her spouse. Given the unique challenges ministers' kids face while "growing up in a fishbowl," elders should keep a special eye out for a minister's family. Just as every member of the body needs relationships that nurture them spiritually, even our senior evangelists need spiritual input and encouragement. As their shepherd, elders can make sure these needs are met.

The Eldership Team

Within the eldership, there are a variety of gifts and experiences that create a balanced team. Of course, having more than one elder is the first step. The scriptural evidence supporting a plurality in a church eldership is extensive. The following chronologically listed passages refer to elders in the plural:[5]

- The *elders* in Jerusalem (Acts 11:30)
- "Let them call the *elders* of the church." (James 5:14)
- "Paul and Barnabas appointed *elders* for them in each church." (Acts 14:23)
- The apostles and *elders* in Jerusalem (Acts 15:2, 4, 6, 22, 23)
- "Paul sent to Ephesus for the *elders* of the church." (Acts 20:17)
- "Keep watch over yourselves and all the flock of which the Holy Spirit has made you *overseers*." (Acts 20:28)
- "Be *shepherds* of the church of God." (Acts 20:28)
- "All the *elders* were present." (Acts 21:18)
- "The *elders* who direct the affairs of the church." (1 Timothy 5:17)
- "Appoint *elders* in every town." (Titus 1:5–6)

In his book on elders, Alexander Strauch writes: "On the local church level, the New Testament plainly witnesses to a consistent

---

[5] Gene Getz, *Elders and Leaders: God's Plan for Leading the Church* (Moody Publishers, 2003), 209-210).

pattern of shared pastoral leadership. Therefore, leadership by a plurality of elders is a sound biblical practice."[6]

Benefits of Shared Leadership Among Elders

Developing an effective team of elders requires much more than simply appointing more than one elder. Forging a team requires intentionality, hard work, and humility. It will not simply happen—it requires sacrificing time, crucifying pride, and putting on sincere mutual love. The reward is well worth the effort, as there are many blessings of a highly functioning eldership. Strauch mentions three primary benefits of developing such a team:[7]

Balancing weaknesses: Elders should be the first to admit that they have weaknesses. Some are prone to legalism, some tend toward sentimentality, some are weak in confrontation, some are not as gifted in encouragement. A healthy eldership team corrects for such weaknesses through the natural strengths of others, mitigating the potential negative impact of an individual's weakness on the church.

Sharing the load: Elders are called by God to engage, protect, and nurture the flock. This is tough work. Our brothers and sisters often look to us to provide comfort in the hardest of times and hope in the darkest of circumstances. Difficult decisions are required that will significantly affect lives, individually or collectively as a church. In light of our own humanity it is essential for elders to be able to lean on one another. We need each other's wisdom, insight, and encouragement. Sharing the load also means that elders can take periods of sabbatical rest to stay refreshed. There are always needs in the church, but knowing others are available helps an elder to step away when seasons of life demand such a need..

Being accountable: Elders are sinners, too. We can be tempted by pride, anger, or bitterness. We need brothers in our lives who can provide inspirational examples and probing care to protect our hearts.

These benefits only result when elders are committed to deep and authentic relationships. An eldership team should be more than an

---

[6] Alexander Strauch, *Biblical Eldership: An Urgent Call to Restore Biblical Church Leadership* (Colorado Springs, CO: Lewis and Roth, 2010), 37.

[7] Strauch, 40–43.

advisory board or business board. Elders should lead the way in mutual vulnerability and openness. As someone said, our spirituality is the ceiling of the church.

Different Gifts, Equal Value

Within an eldership team, different gifts and experiences will and should be represented. The classic passage in Romans 12:3–8 illustrates how Christ's body is made up of members with a wide array of gifts. So it is with the eldership. Some are gifted at teaching, others at serving, some at compassion, others have leadership. None of these is more important than any other, so it is important to be humble in recognizing one's own gifts and acknowledging those of others (verse 3). One of the pitfalls of shared leadership, even within the eldership team, is that we can fail to acknowledge these differences.

I have heard it said that step one of a great team is to get the right people on the bus. But step two is just as critical: making sure team members sit in the right seats. Sometimes our reluctance to honestly discuss our gifts can lead to ambiguity and lack of clear responsibilities. This can lead to ineffectiveness at best, and frustration and even disunity at worst. Again, no gift is better than another, and God provides our abilities so that as a team we can be the best possible servants and shepherds for his people.

A few thoughts:

- It can be helpful for an eldership to discuss the basic areas in which all the elders will serve. Ezekiel 34 paints a clear picture of the pastoral care inherent in our shepherding role. Strengthening the weak, healing the sick, binding up the injured, and searching for strays are activities that should be reflected in the lives of all elders. Practically speaking, an eldership team can discuss how to handle the need to pray for those who are weak or sick, visit those who are hospitalized, or meet with those who are struggling spiritually. These are areas in which every elder plays a part through prayer and action.

- Elders should have the humility to acknowledge and respect the various gifts and skill sets represented on the team. For example, an elder may have the gift of administration (1 Corinthians 12:28 NASB), which enables him to help with church planning and organization. Another may have the gift of encouragement and can help ensure that relationships are deep within the leadership team and the church. Elders with the gift of teaching can help ground planning and decision making in the Word. Recognizing these gifts does not limit an elder to only serving in one specific capacity, but it certainly does help make sure that any "holes" in the leadership team are recognized and accounted for.

- Romans 12 refers to the gift of leadership. The eldership is a team of equals, men who each bring much needed faith, experience, and skill to the church. However, as with any team, leadership is a key component to effectiveness. Whether through "election" among the elders or simply through honest discussion, it is always important that a certain elder (or elders) be acknowledged as the "leader among leaders" or "first among equals." If there are several with the gift of leadership, this role can be structured as a leadership rotation to avoid burnout or insular thinking. Humble and gifted leadership will help ensure progress in planning, decision making, and strategy, which will benefit the eldership, the church leadership, and the entire church.

Ultimately, every elder must be more committed to meeting the church's needs than they are to their own preferences. What does the church need? How can I best be used? Who is best for this role? How can I support this team? These are questions that an elder must humbly grapple with in prayer and in counsel with those who know him well.

Flexibility in Shared Leadership

Many of us enjoy the thrill and passion of organized sports. If we pay attention, we also recognize that a successful coaching staff is able to adjust their strategy in order to optimize the various talents represented on their team roster at any given time. There are abundant examples of a coach stubbornly insisting upon a specific game plan despite the team's lack of talent to execute that plan. When a coaching staff is able to blend the reality of their roster with their strategic principles, a winning season is often the result.

As overseers of the church, elders should likewise show flexibility in how the shared leadership of the church operates. As stated earlier, elders are responsible for outcomes. Is the church growing? Is it healthy? Are we fulfilling God's vision for the body of Christ? At the same time, there is no single leadership "structure" that is best for every situation.

For example, in some churches the full-time ministry staff is very mature both in life and in ministry experience. The eldership may delegate most ministry planning, strategy, and execution to the staff and focus primarily on general pastoral care and specific activities such as family ministry or counseling. In other churches, the leadership may be gifted but less experienced. Here, the eldership may take a larger role in the planning and development of strategy, or helping in teaching. As the shared leadership team develops and matures, this balance should shift over time to reflect growing skill sets and experience, as well as the addition of any new members to the team.

Scripturally, the eldership will always remain accountable to God for the direction and growth of the church. How to get there is an ongoing conversation among the shared leadership team that requires absolute submission to Christ, respect for biblical principles, and mutual love and respect.

Chapter Eight

ELDERS AS FAMILY BUILDERS IN GOD'S CHURCH, PART 1

Sam Laing

> Both the one who makes people holy and those who are made holy are of the same family. So Jesus is not ashamed to call them brothers and sisters. (Hebrews 2:11)

> He must manage his own family well... If anyone does not know how to manage his own family, how can he take care of God's church? (1 Timothy 3:4–5)

> "A new command I give you: Love one another. As I have loved you, so you must love one another. By this everyone will know that you are my disciples, if you love one another." (John 13:34–35)

God intends for us, as his church, to be his family. Did he send Jesus here to save us but then leave us in isolation? No! His desire is that we be born again, become his children, and be close to him. We are born into a family with his other children as well—a family where we, as brothers and sisters, learn to love one another.

What has mankind done to alter this plan? How has the world departed from the clear teaching of God? Look around and observe the answers to these questions. The vast majority of groups bearing the name "church" are far from being a warm, close family. Instead, they are merely Sunday morning events that people visit and then leave, without having Christ-centered, spiritual, and lifechanging relationships of intimate, loving closeness to one another.

As followers of Christ and as those seeking to restore the teachings of the Bible in our lives and in God's church, let us determine and learn how to build a church with a membership that truly loves God our Father and also loves one another as his family of born-again brothers and sisters.

How is this going to happen? How will God bring this about?

Here is his plan: he wants elders—men who are proven to be skilled at building their own families—to serve in a vital role of building that same kind of close, spiritual family culture in his church. This is why, at the heart of God's qualifications for eldership as revealed in Scripture, is the proven ability to build an intimate, holy family.

This begins with a man being a faithful child of God—one who loves his Father in Heaven and is close to him, and who is an obedient and faithful disciple living under the lordship of Jesus. But then it goes beyond this wonderful foundation to another wonderful place—the building of a great family.

To do this, a man must be both a good husband and a good father. Let's look at what it takes to be each of these, as revealed to us in the Word. This will tell us how God wants such men to serve as family builders in his beloved church, the body of Christ.

Elders as Husbands

> For the husband is the head of the wife as Christ is the head of the church, his body... Husbands, love your wives, just as Christ loved the church and gave himself up for her to make her holy, cleansing her by the washing with water through the word, and to present her to himself as a radiant church, without stain or wrinkle or any other blemish, but holy and blameless. (Ephesians 5:23, 25–27)

How is Jesus' relationship to his church described in the passage above? The church is his wife, and he is her husband. (See also Revelation 19:6–8.) So it is no surprise that to be an elder, a man must not only have a wife, but also have the united relationship with her that

God has commanded. As he and his wife work together, they will be able to build a family that is godly, spiritual, and loving.

What are men told to do in order to be the husbands that God calls them to be? God, in the passage quoted above, reveals two vital items: husbands are to *love* and to *lead*.

Elders: Loving Husbands, and Lovers of God's Church

Let's look at Paul's inspired teaching on how husbands are to love their wives and reflect upon how this can help us as elders know even better how we are to love the church, the bride of Christ.

Initiatory lovers

Jesus *initiated* love to us in order to save us, calling us to follow him. And now that we are members of his church, his bride, he continues to do so.

So what does this mean that we, as elders, need to do to show love to the church?

It means that we, as servants and imitators of Jesus, must initiate love to his bride, the church, just as we have done with our own wives. Brothers, let us be inspiring originators of the expression of love in God's family. Let us be the ones who reach out and love first, who love consistently, and who show the most love in all of his household! To do this, we must spend time with people—time listening to them, feeling with them, and encouraging them as they live their lives. God's church will then see a flesh-and-blood example of initiatory love—an example that enables them to see in living color the love of God their Father, and of Jesus, the husband of the church.

Since this world is separated from Christ, most people have not experienced in their families the kind of love that God longs for them to see. So, brothers, we need to sow seeds of love in our church family, initiating love with our members as we do with our wives and children, "because he first loved us" (1 John 4:19). As we initiate the love of God through our words, deeds, interactions, and warm affection, this love will soon take root in the lives of our church members and spread throughout the family.

Sacrificial Lovers

> Husbands, love your wives, just as Christ loved the church and gave himself up for her. (Ephesians 5:25, emphasis added)

We are called to love our wives *sacrificially*—just as Jesus has loved us and his church. He paid a great price to demonstrate his love. What is the result of this sacrificial demonstration of love? His love transforms our lives and gives us a wonderful relationship with him. With that same spirit of selfless sacrifice, we can—and should—love the members of the church of Jesus!

Only Jesus, the sinless Son of God, could die on the cross to redeem his church. But what can we, as elders, do to help build it? We can imitate the sacrificial spirit of Jesus, bringing into his church the same kind of unselfish love we have for our wives. As a result God's church will grow in holiness and radiance (see Ephesians 5:25–27).

Brothers, we have won and will retain the hearts of our wives by our love. Jesus did the same for us in the most sacrificial and powerful way ever seen. As we bring the same spirit of love into the family of God that we have brought into the lives of our wives, the church will feel the love of Jesus in a face-to-face, warm, and personal manner as they experience our love for them as their elders.

Sensitive Lovers

> In this same way, husbands *ought to love their wives as their own bodies. He who loves his wife loves himself. After all, no one ever hated his own body, but they feed and care for their body, just as Christ does the church.* (Ephesians 5:28–29, emphasis added)

A husband is to love his wife as he loves himself—as he loves his own body. What does this mean? When our body is hungry, we feed it. When our body is tired, we rest it. When our body is in pain, we seek to relieve it. As husbands, we are "one flesh" with our wives, and we are to love her in this sensitive manner. Of course, we can't be "one flesh" with the members of our church—that unique relationship is for us and our wives alone! But what we can do is to bring that kind of love into our church as we feel for our members with a deep sensitivity to their needs. What are ways we can show this love to the church?

Is someone hurting? Are they weary? Are they spiritually weak and malnourished? Are they feeling out of touch and lonely? Then let's love them by sensing their needs and reaching out to them ourselves, and by assisting them to build relationships with other caring disciples who can be their ongoing friends and helpers.

Is someone doing well spiritually? Are they loving, compassionate, humble and gentle, and are they helping others by teaching and admonishing them with wisdom? (Colossians 3:12–16). Then let's commend them, encourage them, and help them to continue to help others in the church who need what they have to give.

Elders: Loving Leadership through Example and Teaching

> For the husband is the head of the wife as Christ is the head of the church, his body, of which he is the Savior. (Ephesians 5:23)

This passage tells us that Jesus is the head of his church and also her Savior. This means that Jesus is both the leader of the church, and her "lover" well (Ephesians 5:25).

We as husbands have proven ourselves to be loving leaders of our wives. We have led them spiritually by setting an example for them in our walk with God. They have seen our hunger for him—our efforts to trust, to obey, and to be close to him in prayer and consistent Bible study. We have not only helped them by demonstrating a godly example, but also as we have taught and shared with them the word of God—helping them apply it in practical, real ways in their character and daily lives. Likewise, they have helped us apply the Scriptures to our lives.

May we do the same for the church, the bride of Christ. Let us lead by our life example and as we teach and train the church, both in group and personal settings. This is how we imitate the loving leadership of

Jesus, who led by example in these same ways. Leading in both of these ways not only helps individuals but builds family as well.

For what purpose and in what direction do we lead? We lead the bride of Christ so that she can be holy and close to God, so that she can grow spiritually and in knowledge, and so that she can keep her faith and go to heaven. May we as elders love by leading and lead by loving. Yes, brothers, may we lead the church, the bride of Christ, as we have sought to lead our own wives...in a loving and sacrificial way!

Loving Leadership: Respectful and Considerate

> *Husbands, in the same way be considerate as you live with your wives, and treat them with respect* as the weaker partner and as heirs with you of the gracious gift of life, so that nothing will hinder your prayers. (1 Peter 3:7, emphasis added)

Leadership can often carry connotations of disrespect and condescending attitudes, as well as inconsiderate and impersonal interactions. God does not relate to us like this, and we should not relate to others in this way. As husbands, we are the "head" of our wives, but that does not mean we are superior to them in the eyes of God, or that we are to be bossy and harsh. Instead, we are to be considerate, caring, kind, and humble.

Let us lead our churches, but in a kind and godly manner, being loving, considerate, and respectful, just as we are with our wives. To be considerate of our wives means we seek to study their needs and be sympathetic to how they are feeling. Being considerate of the church means that we, as leaders, are to imitate Jesus in his loving leadership. He is certainly our leader, but he knows how we feel and is deeply compassionate toward us. (See Hebrews 2:10–18; 4:14–5:2.)

Peter, in the passage quoted at the beginning of this section, also tells us that we are to be respectful of our wives. We are the head of our wives (Ephesians 5:23), but this does not mean we are identical to our Lord Jesus in his position as the head of the church. God has placed us as husbands in a leadership role, but unlike Jesus, we are not superior in nature—we and our wives are equal before God. We lead them, all the while knowing that we are of matching value, and that we ourselves are under God's authority. In the same way, let us assertively lead the church, all the while respecting our members, not regarding them as inferior to us or of lesser value before our God.

In summary…let's be *loving leaders:*

- Let us, in love, lead our churches forward—taking them higher and higher as the bride of Christ, and as the children and family of God.
- Let's love those we lead as we love ourselves (and our own bodies!) by being sensitive to them, aware of how they are feeling, and what they are going through.
- Let's lead them with consideration and respect, knowing that we are all under the lordship of Christ.

Elders as Fathers

Elders are not only good and godly husbands for their wives, they are good and godly fathers to their children. So, brothers, what can we as elders learn from raising our own kids? What wisdom can we take from our experience as fathers and use to build a family culture in God's church?

Love Your Children

We are good fathers because we have loved our children as we have been loved by God and by Jesus:

> We love because he first loved us. (1 John 4:19)

> "My command is this: Love each other as I have loved you." (John 15:12)

We have loved each one of our children. We have spent time with them and come to know them—their hearts, their needs, their weaknesses, and their strengths. We have sought to be close to them even when at times it may have been difficult to do so. This is what made us good fathers!

Do Not Exasperate Your Children

> Fathers, do not exasperate your children; instead, bring them up in the training and instruction of the Lord. (Ephesians 6:4)

How do we exasperate our own children? Exasperation can often happen when:

- They feel that by our actions or attitudes we are violating what we have been teaching them; that when we do or say something wrong or inappropriate, we do not see it or admit it, apologize, and ask for their forgiveness. (Exasperation of this nature can also occur when they see us behave in the same manner toward other family members.)

- We lose our temper and are harsh, rude, and insensitive to their feelings.

- They feel we ignore them, fail to truly listen to them, or just do all of the talking ourselves.

- We don't explain what we are saying as we lead them; we just say it and expect them to do it. (This obviously is more of an issue as the years go by and our children become more mature and thoughtful.)

- We expect compliance to our leadership but are not relationally close to them and are not consistently or warmly expressive of our love.

- We focus on the "outside," just on their behavior, and do not have heart-to-heart talks that help us sense how they are feeling and what they are thinking.

- We do not recognize and commend them for the good that they do; we do not encourage them when they are struggling and suffering.

Nurture, Train, and Instruct Them in the Lord

In the verse cited in the previous section (Ephesians 6:4), God (speaking through the Apostle Paul) tells fathers how to bring up their children. The Greek word translated as "bring…up" has as its deeper meaning the concept of nurturing. As we nurture our children, we are also told to do two more things: to give them "the training and instruction of the Lord."

What do these three concepts mean, and how do they fit together?

- To nurture means to *feed* our children with the word of God by sharing it on a *heart and mind* level, teaching it to them from their earliest days into their teen years. (See Deuteronomy 6:4–7.)
- God calls upon us as fathers to not deal with our children impersonally, but to invest our hearts and time so that we may connect with them emotionally and spiritually. He wants us to provide consistent warmth and affection as we nurture, teach, and train them.
- Nurturing, teaching, and training is to be done by using the word of God as our resource and by showing how it has specifically applied to our own lives, and applies to theirs as well.
- Nurturing, training, and teaching from the Bible helps them to see that the most important matters we teach are based not on our personal opinions, but on the word of God.
- As we teach and train them, we need to draw them out by asking questions and carefully listening, in order to learn what they are thinking and how they are feeling (Proverbs 20:5).
- As we teach, train, and nurture our children we have vision for them and their future—helping them discover and put to use their gifts and talents (Romans 12:6–8).

- We are to believe the best of them and encourage them even when they are struggling with weaknesses and have made mistakes.
- We teach and train them how to be close to their mothers and their siblings. We help them learn how to resolve conflict, how to apologize, and how to forgive when they have been hurt or wronged.
- We pray with them and sing and worship together as a family.
- We smile *at* them and *with* them.

In Closing

Brothers, let's go through the lists above and apply them appropriately as we build family in our local churches. Even though our church members are not in the identical place in our lives as our wives and children, we are to treat them like family and teach them to treat each other that way. We need to spend consistent time helping the church to grow by nurturing, teaching, and training about love, family, and closeness. Let's build family in the body of Christ by putting the heart and principles we learned as husbands and fathers into the church culture, just as God would have us do.

Chapter Nine

ELDERS AS FAMILY BUILDERS IN GOD'S CHURCH, PART 2
Sam Laing

> For this reason I kneel before the Father, from whom every family in heaven and on earth derives its name. (Ephesians 3:14–15)

> Therefore, as we have opportunity, let us do good to all people, especially to those who belong to the family of believers. (Galatians 6:10)

God wants us as elders to bring into *his* family the good principles we lived and built in *our* families. We set that example in our own homes, but how can we make it happen in the church? How can we "see to it" (Hebrews 12:15) in a practical manner? How can we as elders build a close family culture in the church when its membership is quite large—so numerous that we cannot give every member the kind of personal attention that we gave to our wives and to each of our own children?

Intimacy in a Large Fellowship

Since the church is to be a loving, intimate family, does this mean that its membership should be small—that there should not be a large number of disciples coming together for fellowship?

As we can see in the history God has preserved for us in the book of Acts, there are examples of large numbers of people being baptized into Christ and being in the same church. While we are not given the precise details of how they functioned, we know that at times they all met together to worship, and they also met in each other's homes. To put it simply: they met in large assemblies, and they also met in small groups. (See Acts 2:42–47; 6:1–6; 14:26–28; 15:30; 18:7–8; 19:8–10, and more.)

There are great benefits to both large and small sessions of assembly. Large groups of people gathering brings us special and unique blessings. When we see disciples by the dozens, hundreds, or more in an assembly, it can create an immense sense of inspiration for us all. It also gives a great opportunity for powerful public preaching and magnificent worship. Nothing supersedes the energy of a substantial crowd singing together. When people, whether members or visitors, come in our door and see a large and diverse community in age, race, background, and culture they are amazed, inspired, and moved by the power of God and his Son to lovingly unite people who, in this world, are tragically estranged from one another.

Certainly, large numbers of souls in worship assembly can bring unique blessings to our churches.

But large assembly alone does not build family. If this is the only way our church comes together, we cannot and will not build a church with close and loving relationships. To enjoy family relationships in the church we must build intimate, close, smaller groups within our fellowship.

If our church is large in number, and the disciples cannot personally know or be known to everyone else in the membership, how can we build (or be) a family?

Here are some practical suggestions to consider so that we, as elders who have built our own intimate families, can lead the way in creating intimacy in God's family—his church.

Building Family in Church through Small Groups

How big are most families? How big was yours?

There is no set number, but it is obvious that God designed families to be small enough so that every family member could receive personal attention and be close to everyone else.

We must create small groups so that every member in our larger church family will have an intimate circle of friends through which they can both receive and give the individual attention, encouragement, and training that God intends. So, let's build small, intimate families within the larger, expansive membership of God's church.

How can we build a sufficient number of effective smaller families within the larger church family?

Select and train leaders

As elders, we are told by God to "equip the saints for the work of ministry" (Ephesians 4:12 ESV). This means that by training willing and capable members how to lead small groups we can build a numerically large church that still has an intimate family culture. Let's reach out to our membership, seeking and finding members who have the heart and capability to do this, and then train them how.

Individually shepherd the leaders

Once members are appointed as family group leaders, let's be sure that we as elders are shepherding them as they help us to shepherd the flock. We need to organize the ongoing training of these leaders so that each one receives continued individual instruction by one of the elders on our team, or by another skilled person that at least one of us is connected to and has assigned to that role.

Personal attention by elders to family group leaders will also help them be able to successfully deal with the burdens that accompany the blessings of building a family. Those who are leading our small groups can easily become overwhelmed by the sheer amount of energy it takes. Elders, let's be there to help them bear the burden, and let's give them the wisdom and encouragement they need.

As we shepherd them, we also need to listen to them with wisdom. We must seek to fully understand what they (and their group) are feeling and experiencing. We need to hear their ideas on ways to build family, and not just dictate our ideas to them. Why do we need to listen to them? This will help us understand the particular needs of the Christians they serve, and how they think they can best meet those needs. This is especially important as we, as older men, work with younger leaders and groups. We must grasp, from their point of view, the challenges and pragmatics involved in building their particular group into one that is both spiritual and evangelistically fruitful. As we listen to them we will become more effective in advising and equipping them (in their generation's culture) to teach unchanging biblical principles, practices, and doctrine, even while using fresh (godly and wise) methods.

Visit the groups

As we shepherd and train the small group leaders, we should also visit their groups frequently enough to see how they are doing. As we do this, we will be able to give wise and needed input to the group leaders and get closer to more members of our church. Because of our visits, both the leader and the group members will feel the security, confidence, and encouragement that come from having ongoing family times with an elder.

Help them utilize the talents within their group and raise up new leaders.

We need to teach our small group leaders that they are not to bear the whole responsibility of leadership themselves. Let's encourage and assist them to raise up other members who do their part in helping to care for and build their family—just as we did with our own children.

It is very important that new leaders are continually being raised up within the groups. Why is this necessary? Think about this reality of family life. Our kids, when they marry, leave us to build their own families (Genesis 2:22–24). Our family groups will go through a similar version of this process. As they grow in number (and maturity) they will need to divide and form smaller families once again so that they can maintain the closeness that comes from a manageable number of members. So as we raise up and equip new leaders, our groups will be able to apportion into smaller, more intimate groups that can retain the same family spirit they had before their numbers increased and things started getting impersonal.

Oversee the groups as a team

We as elders should work closely with one another and with the ministry staff to evaluate the effectiveness of the family culture in the entire church. We will need wisdom, advice, and encouragement as we seek to equip those who lead and oversee their groups, striving to help all their members grow and mature.

Address and assist in conflict resolution

We will need to teach publicly and counsel privately concerning ways to resolve conflicts that can occur between our members and within our family groups. We learned to be peacemakers in our marriages and among our own children…so now, let's use what we learned to help others do the same.

Teach marriage and parenting

And, one last bit of advice on family building: as elders, let's do lots of teaching on marriage and parenting to families in our churches, since we have a history of good outcomes in this area. Of course, neither we nor our families were (or are) perfect—but we learned from God and his word how to build them and make Jesus Lord in the process. As we share what we have learned, it will help the marriages and families in our church to grow, to overcome, to become sources of encouragement to our membership, and to be examples in our communities of the wisdom and power of God.

Great Results Happen When Elders Build Family in the Church

Let us realize that it is through building small groups that give individual attention to church members that we can fulfill Jesus' command to "make disciples…baptizing them in the name of the Father, the Son and the Holy Spirit, and teaching them to obey everything I have commanded you" (Matthew 28:19–20). If we create, maintain, and nourish such groups, not only will our members and churches grow spiritually, but they will also grow in number. As people see the gospel being lived out in love among us, they will be drawn to follow Jesus.

May we focus on this wonderful command and promise from Jesus and seek to shepherd and lead his flock to this destination:

> "A new command I give you: Love one another. As I have loved you, so you must love one another. By this everyone will

know that you are my disciples, if you love one another." (John 13:34–35)

Brothers, as we build loving family in our churches, our members—as well as countless people in the world around us—will behold the power and love of God in our fellowship, and their lives will be forever changed!

Chapter Ten

WORKING DYNAMICS OF AN ELDERSHIP
Wyndham Shaw

An eldership is only as strong as its unity and ability to work together. Spiritual and successful dynamics don't happen by accident. They must be striven for and maintained. Honesty, humility, listening, learning, and growing are key elements for elders to contribute to a great working dynamic.

1 Corinthians 5:6 tells us that "a little yeast leavens the whole batch of dough." A modern proverb similarly states, "One bad apple spoils the bunch."

May we never be that "bad apple" who makes group functioning difficult.

I have shared in many workshops important principles of group dynamics I've gained (and added to) from Bill Hybels' book, *Axiom: Powerful Leadership Proverbs,* where he writes about "three C's" of leadership: character, competency, and chemistry.[8] I have added a fourth, conviction.

Healthy group dynamics are best attained when we pay attention to our group's conviction, character, competence, and chemistry. Since other chapters in this book cover conviction, character, and competence, the focus of this chapter will be chemistry. (I am referring to the way we work together—how we "play with others on the playground.")

We must ask ourselves (and others, since we often don't clearly see our strengths and weaknesses) if our personal dynamics within a group produce a damaging chemical explosion, don't change anything,

---

[8] Bill Hybels, *Axiom: Powerful Leadership Proverbs* (Grand Rapids, MI: Zondervan, 2008).

or blend elements that result in something wonderful.

What's It Like to Work with Me?

Our elders once had an exercise where each elder asked the question of the others, "What's it like to work with me?"

It was encouraging and challenging. While I received much encouragement, I learned that I talked too much. Since I had been an elder for the longest, others were tempted to not speak up, or when speaking up were overly strong, to prove to themselves or to others that they would be heard. This realization was eye-opening for me—convicting me to listen more carefully and to speak less quickly. I knew the scripture that taught this lesson in James 1:19; I just did not realize how applicable it was to me!

We are often blind to the ways we are viewed in a group setting. It's important to be open to each other and learn from each other how to grow in our group dynamics. We must never allow elephants to sit in our living rooms. (For any who are not familiar with this terminology, an "elephant in the room" is an expression referring to an awkward or even sinful dynamic [the elephant] that looms large and is obvious to everyone but is ignored.) Unfortunately, fear of conflict often leaves that elephant in the room undiscussed yet wreaking havoc on relational and working dynamics. We must learn to practice Ephesians 4:15, speaking the truth in love.

Common Sense Communication

A common relationship problem mentioned in the Scriptures is misunderstanding due to lack of communication. Consider the two tribes who almost went to war in Joshua 22 because they made assumptions of each other's motives without communicating. Similar problems of misunderstanding, conflict, and hurt happen today, but they can often be avoided if communication lines are open. It's hard to overcommunicate, but all too easy to undercommunicate—especially when we assume others know what we know or think the way we think. None of us like surprises caused by lack of communication.

Whenever our elders meet, we find it important to follow a clear process of communication. This begins with an understanding of who is to communicate what, who should be communicated to, and in what order it should happen. Our eldership has learned the value of gathering an agenda for any and all meetings. This practice invites inclusiveness, with all elders having a chance to contribute. The agenda manager can then order the topics by importance, relevancy, and urgency.

Agendas should be sent out ahead of time. This way, each elder can be prepared with any needed work and can ask for clarification to shed light on any topic before the meetings.

Elders should possess the integrity to respond to emails promptly and to contribute to the agenda when they have something that needs the elders' attention. Our personal negligence can slow the entire group process.

Can We Have Some Fun and Fellowship Here?

Without good planning our meetings can become dry and long—tempting us to disengage. When Jesus met together with his disciples, food and prayer were often involved. Jesus knows that intimacy is often built through eating together—accompanied with prayer. Our eldership begins our meeting time by sharing a meal together (which one of the couples brings—we take turns). We then include a time of good news and prayer. We desperately need God's involvement in our times together. Years ago, one of the elders encouraged us to include short prayers throughout the meetings, continually asking God for his wisdom and blessings on our discussions and decisions. This has been a wise practice, reminding us of our dependence on God for his wisdom and his promise to provide needed wisdom.

We have found it extremely valuable to include our wives in our meetings. They share in the meals, share in the prayers, and bring valuable discussion and contribution to the meetings. They take responsibility for their humble and gracious composure (as do we). Given our conviction of elders having responsibility for oversight, they don't take part in any voting.

How Do We Make Decisions?

One of the common mistakes leaders make is to discuss, discuss, and discuss some more—without making decisions and executing actions that result in completed tasks. We need time for prayer, for biblical application, and for the Holy Spirit to guide us, but then we need to act.

Action items and clarity about who is responsible for executing those items must be clearly understood. Some form of accountability, along with a stated deadline, contributes toward our ability to make progress.

When we need to gather more information in order to complete a task, we create a task force who will, after their work, give feedback to the whole group. Time and wisdom do not allow us to be equally involved in researching all decisions that must be made, so delegating the workload assures that appropriate factors are considered.

Those most affected by decisions should have an opportunity to share their thoughts about those decisions. Two questions are important to answer in the decision-making process: Have all the relevant people been heard? And have all the relevant discussions of the facts happened? We must learn to be good, observant, and inclusive listeners.

Solomon shares such wisdom when he states in Ecclesiastes 12:13, "Now all has been heard; here is the conclusion of the matter…"

After all has been heard, it's good and right to come to a conclusion.

The "Jethro Principle" and "The Matrix"

Our past failures concerning process forced our eldership to initiate a decision-making matrix.

Careful and orderly communication can help lessen hurtful mistakes in decision making. We need excellent forethought to apply the appropriate scope and order of presentations as we make and communicate decisions. These types of decisions and corresponding conversations would include:

Major decisions that affect the whole church: In these decisions it's important to decide who will lead the process, who should be consulted, and who needs to be involved in the final approval. When communicating changes that could affect the entire church, it is of utmost importance to make sure the elders, evangelists, teachers, women leaders, and family group leaders are informed and united.

An example of this type of communication was done in the Boston church several years ago when the elders decided that in order to shepherd the church and see to it that needs were met, every member should be in a small group. While this had been the practice for many years, we wanted to renew our commitment to this needed function. We discussed this process with the elders and staff, and then the family group leaders, and then the congregation.

Major decisions that affect a smaller portion of the church: These would likely be led by the leaders most involved with that portion of the church, with the elders being informed.

Major decisions might include those that take the whole church or region in a different direction, including church discipline, personnel, and budget.

Minor decisions: These need the same planning of who "takes point" in the consideration, decisions, and communication processes. In these types of decisions, usually the elders only need to be informed. If the elders become overinvolved in decisions that are better assessed by smaller groups, they will frustrate the leaders of those groups by failing to give them enough trust. They will also wear themselves out by becoming involved in too many decisions. Moses' father-in-law, Jethro, taught Moses the importance of delegation in Exodus 18. Elders should know how to apply the "Jethro principle" well. Minor decisions would not include changes to strategy, personnel, or budget but might include things such as staff discipling, all-church calendars, and other items.

Administrative issues such as budgets, financial decisions outside of the budget, and issues related to human resources all need the same attention to a decision-making matrix. Elders should strive to keep themselves and the ministers focused on prayer, ministry of the Word, and taking care of the flock instead of becoming distracted by administrative details. A vital part of any ministry is following the scriptural directives in Romans 12:4–8, which instruct us that each disciple is to use their gifts. This is not only important for each disciple, but essential for the functioning of the church. As elders, we must let them exercise their gifts.

These details have been helpful tools for our eldership—leading to more focused and timely decisions accompanied by appropriate communication.

How Does an Eldership Stay United When Everyone Does Not Agree?

You may likely remember a time, years ago, when your children were young and you asked them where they would like to go to eat. Chances are, you got many different answers, even from within one relatively small family. People are different. We think differently and come from different backgrounds, cultures, and perspectives—thus we don't always agree.

Likewise, an eldership will have different points of view on various topics that are not clear biblical directives. We may feel strongly about our point of view and wonder why others can't see our perspective—the "right" one. (We would do well to remember the importance of accepting our brothers and sisters when it comes to disputable matters.) Remember those qualities of character that are imperative for elders? They also apply when we disagree with each other! We must listen to each other's perspective, seeking to understand more than seeking to be understood. We must learn to be persuadable, and also learn to persuade. We must strive to be completely humble and gentle (Ephesians 4:2).

Persuading and Being Persuadable

In the book of Acts we see Gamaliel persuading the Sanhedrin to spare the lives of Peter and the other apostles. Paul's words persuaded many to turn to Jesus, and Lydia's persuasive words changed the travel plans of Paul and his fellow disciples, convincing them to stay at her house. Other biblical accounts show some who opposed the gospel persuading crowds to oppose Jesus and his disciples.

Persuasion is neither right nor wrong in itself—it is only persuasion. The subject matter for which we are seeking to persuade our hearers may be a matter of right or wrong or may be opinion. It's necessary to ascertain the difference.

Our words and our example are powerful tools of persuasion.

When we feel strongly about a need within the church or a topic related to functioning in the church, we can certainly try to persuade others to see our point of view. However, to be obedient to the Scriptures, we must be completely humble and gentle as we do so, treating each other with love and respect. Our logic and understanding may persuade others, or it may not. We must seek to be at peace with either outcome.

Humility is vital as we seek to persuade, and it is vital as we seek to be persuadable. If we can never (or seldom) be persuaded to accept another's point of view, our humility needs to increase.

As we practice persuading and being persuadable in our eldership, we find that decisions seldom come to a vote. Usually we are all persuaded one way or another. However, at times we have differing opinions, so decisions are made by a vote.

Our eldership has decided on a majority rule. Other elderships may function differently, but the method of function should be clear to all. This calls for humility and unity when a decision does not go our way, or even when it does go our way. If it does not, and there is not a clear-cut biblical directive, we would be wrong to "do our own thing." Group dynamics are destroyed by "mavericks," "I told you so-ers," and those with an "us-versus-them" mentality.

When we decide something as an eldership, we decide as one. We leave the room united, even if a decision does not go our way. We don't say, "The others feel one way, but I think differently." We speak as one voice. We choose not to disclose who was for and who was against a decision. While we must be honest, we must be careful to protect our unity.

Each elder should allow themselves to be accountable to the rest of the group. The chairman should take responsibility for ensuring adherence to the agreed-upon operating principles. If one elder becomes an annoyance to the other elders, it is important to talk with him rather than about him with each other. There are times when we may need to call for resolution of a conflict within the group. It is wise to take this "offline" (so as to not disrupt the meeting), but then later reassure the group when resolution has been attained.

In the book Gordon Ferguson and I wrote entitled *Golden Rule Leadership,* we encouraged a consensus leadership style for churches mature enough to have leadership teams with evangelists, elders, and teachers.

Decisions Are Tough

I find that a common deterrent for men qualified to be elders is the responsibility and difficulty they foresee in making tough decisions. This process can also sober those who do become elders. While elders must build unity and shepherd the church, they cannot shy away from conflict or difficult decisions. And there will be heart-wrenching decisions that at times must be made. Some of the toughest decisions I have been part of as an elder include:

- Marking a personal friend and brotherhood icon
- Laying off or firing a personal friend
- Dealing with factions in the church
- Hiring a lead evangelist
- Responding to angry women with what they did not want to hear
- Responding to angry men with what they did not want to hear
- Laying off greathearted and willing staff for lack of funds
- Making decisions that required predicting the future
- Making decisions that affected my personal family

While decisions and dynamics can at times be challenging, the unity that can be achieved is inspiring and exemplary for all to witness. Confidence comes from our reliance on God's word and his Spirit within. Dynamics in the eldership can truly be dynamic—growing, making progress, and bringing joy instead of burden to all involved.

Chapter Eleven

GUARDING THE FLOCK: ELDERSHIP AND CHURCH DISCIPLINE

Jerry Sugarman and Ron Brumley

Shepherds protect. In fact, at night shepherds would often lie down in the opening of the sheep gate to prevent intruders from coming in or wanderers from going out. Such are also "point men." In his book, *Point Man*, author Steve Farrar compares the duties of a husband and father to that of a point man.[9]

"What is a point man?" you might ask. The point man is the soldier positioned at the head of a military patrol. He spots danger, thus seeking to protect the troops. Those in this position must have the ability to recognize an enemy's booby traps and snares. They are trained to pick out something as small as a glint of light in the foliage or a metallic sheen in the vegetation—signaling the enemy's presence. In the same way, elders are called by God to be spiritual point men for God's church. They must recognize Satan's "booby traps," protect the church from false teachers, and maintain the unity of the flock—especially if the evil one has designs to scatter them through divisiveness and factions.

Guard Against the False Teacher

With this calling in mind, elders must vigorously and proactively protect the flock. In Acts 20:29–32, we are privileged to observe an intimate scene in which the Apostle Paul tells the Ephesian elders to guard the flock from "savage wolves" who "distort the truth." The church in Ephesus was dealing with:

---

[9] Steve Farrar, *Point Man: How a Man Can Lead His Family* (Frisco, Texas: Multnomah Books, 2003).

- Myths, genealogies, speculative intellectualism, controversies, and all kinds of high-sounding nonsense (1 Timothy 1:4, 6–7; 6:20; Titus 3:9)
- Asceticism: laying down special laws (for example, food laws and laws forbidding marriage); listing many things as impure (1 Timothy 4:1–5)
- Failure to provide for one's family (1 Timothy 5:8)
- Greed and gathering money from false teaching (1 Timothy 6:5)
- People denying the coming resurrection (2 Timothy 2:18)
- Quarreling (2 Timothy 2:24–26)
- Men taking advantage of gullible women (2 Timothy 3:6–9)
- Gnosticism: the teaching that all matter is evil and the spirit alone is good—thus, the body and spirit can be separated: "If I'm immoral, it's not really me doing it; it's just my body."

Often, such distortion is subtle: a toxic concoction of spiritual truths covering the hidden lie or self-serving motive. This means elders must be biblically knowledgeable in addition to being "people-wise." Elders need to champion sound doctrine. This means they believe in what might be called spiritual "non-negotiables."

What are some of the foundational doctrines which elders must believe and transmit to the church?

- The inspiration and authority of the Scriptures (2 Timothy 3:16–17)
- God's omniscient, omnipotent, omnipresent, and triune nature (Psalm 147:5; Matthew 28:18–20)
- The deity of Christ (Philippians 2:6)
- The sinless humanity of Jesus (1 Peter 2:22)
- The substitutional death of Jesus (1 Peter 2:24)

- Jesus' physical resurrection, his ascension, and his second coming (Acts 1:9–11)
- Salvation by grace through faith, while recognizing the place baptism has in the conversion process as the starting point of the new birth (Ephesians 2:8–9; Acts 2:38)
- The universal call to evangelize the people of the world and the need for discipleship of all (Matthew 28:18–20)
- A decision to remember the poor (Galatians 2:10)

There are ample matters about which members may rightly have and express opinions, but in the realm of foundational, core doctrines elders are called by God to be strong and decisive. It requires wisdom to know where and when a situation calls for fortitude or freedom. Even greater wisdom is required in liberty, when a person holds tightly to their opinion as if it were a core belief. In these situations the overseer is called to instill in the hearts of members the lesson of valuing people over opinions (Romans 12:10). After being equipped with Scripture, an elder finds his calling in three important areas:

1. Correcting members engaging in false teachings
2. Exposing sinful behavior
3. Keeping secular-cultural drift from creeping into the church

These tools are used for preserving unity and correcting wayward members.

Correcting Members Engaging in False Teachings

Matthew 7:15–16 indicates that one will know wolves in sheep's clothing by identifying their fruit, or the result their lives and teachings produce. Factions, or anything creating disunity in the body of Christ, are an undesired product or fruit. In Titus 3:10 we are instructed to warn a divisive member twice prior to cutting off fellowship.

Exposing Sinful Behavior

Exposing sin is an extremely serious step that elders should oversee. It is actually step three in the four-step process described in Matthew 18:15–17. This passage teaches us that a member who is sinned against is to first confront the offending brother or sister privately. Next, if unity is not achieved through the first step, one or two other disciples are to be brought into the situation. If there is still no listening, understanding, repentance, or humility the "church" must be informed. This stage is aided when facilitated by the skill of a seasoned elder.

Too often, the way we "tell it to the church" is inadequate or without proper context. This should always be considered from the perspective of the amount of influence the transgressor has with the membership. The greater the influence, the larger the number of people who should be informed. Limiting the exposure to the family groups and individuals that are within the sinner's sphere of influence will protect visitors as well as those who may be in the church but are not involved in the matter. It also prevents the name of Jesus from being soiled by indiscriminate public viewing of members' sins.

When all of these efforts are unsuccessful, the fourth and final step in this process is the act of disfellowship. Often, the person will just decide to leave, while other times they love the benefits of the fellowship but don't respect God's word for functioning in the body of Christ, the church. The Scriptures teach that we are to treat the transgressor as a "tax collector." In this context, a tax collector is someone who has betrayed his own people for the benefit of outsiders.

Keeping Secular-Cultural Drift from Creeping into the Church

Cultural morals and ethics decline or degenerate over time, sometimes creating an almost imperceptible drift in the culture of the church. Even with Christians, it may be surprising how much is accepted as morality lessens. A case in point would be the loss of sensitivity by Christians to violence, sex, and profanity in entertainment. People are becoming more and more accustomed to the lack of purity in this area. An elder's sensitivity should be a byproduct of training their thoughts about that which is noble (Philippians 4:8; Hebrews 5:14), and so serve as a standard or moral stronghold that the congregation can look to as an example. An elder's life and teaching should sound a clarion call for

Christians to restore purity and one's first love (Hebrews 13:4; Revelation 2:4–5).

Church Discipline as a Guardrail

Engineers carefully design the strategic placement of guardrails on convoluted mountain roads to prevent vehicles from careening off the highway. Most of the time they are not needed, but their very presence brings security for travelers. In the same way, the precious relationships in the church are like guardrails that keep people from careening off the narrow path. The elder that is relationally integrated into the lives of his flock can most effectively protect the church and help its members to live righteous lives.

Church discipline uses the currency of the fellowship as leverage to challenge a sinning Christian to repent and be reconciled to God and his church. This has, however, been a sore spot in history. Church discipline should serve to bring back a repentant sinner, repair relational damage, and keep the unity of the body. Instead, too often the church, out of sentimentality (or even cowardice), fails to act; or in contrast, discovers that a hurt person is trying to extract "a pound of flesh" from those who have offended them. Grace and truth are always needed, and much prayer is required to administer them in a Christlike way.

Fortunately, in the Apostle Paul's letters to the Corinthians we have an excellent example of a sinner coming to his senses by a church's appropriate response. In 1 Corinthians 5:1–5, and 2 Corinthians 2:5–11 and 7:8–13, we see Paul directing the church. First, he strongly challenges the church to eliminate the grievous sin that exists in their membership. Incest (a son and his stepmother are in an immoral relationship) is being enabled and even celebrated.

Second, Paul gives instructions for church disfellowship, outlining how to do it as well as communicating its purpose. Scripture intimates that Paul wrote a scathing letter in between 1 and 2 Corinthians, upgrading the challenge and most likely hurting some feelings. Paul told the church to turn the sinner over to Satan so that he would miss the fellowship and repent. Finally, in the last letter to the Corinthian church, everyone involved has repented and reconciliation and unity are achieved.

Several key thoughts come from these passages. Church discipline is used to inspire the offender to godliness. It is not intended to subjugate the sinner. Common mistakes made in this area range from enabling sin to overcorrection of the sinner. Bottom line, missing fellowship is meant to prompt repentance—and the congregation and sinner can then grow together in love and unity.

Another important concept we can learn from this example is that there are ingredients necessary in order to be reconciled. The repentant sinner must have godly sorrow (2 Corinthians 7:8–11). Before God and the people they hurt or impacted, they must express sorrow for sin. This must lead them to verbally express their repentance to both God and the church. Thus, the repentant person releases control of the scenario, and the response is now in the hands of the offended. The one offended may choose not to forgive, but this would be that individual's sin before God. God's design, however, is for all involved to yield to unconditional love and forgiveness.

As Paul noted, the Corinthians came to repentance, as shown by their earnestness, eagerness to right the wrong, indignation, alarm, and concern for the present situation as well as for the future. Repentance should result in a conviction to never have this happen again. The wise leader calls on the sinner to express conviction and a plan for change to increase the person's determination to repent, and as an expression of that determination. Keeping the focus and fear of God helps the sinner to gain deep convictions based on their relationship with God.

Reconciling the sinner is an important and necessary component of discipline. While the most important factor is the restoration of the offender to God, the restoration of their relationship to the members of the church is also of great importance. This includes any restitution (the correction of any damage done), and finally the restoration of the joy of fellowship. This, depending on the amount of hurt or emotional damage, can be challenging. An elder can broker the sinner's reentry into the congregation, just like Barnabas did for Saul in Acts 9:26–28. All of this should be part of the elder's duties. The attitudes and emotions present in the restoration of fellowship are modeled in the parable of the prodigal son, as the father expresses exuberant joy in the return of his wayward son. Also, we can learn from Joseph, who when he forgave his brothers, also offered reassurance of his love for them (Genesis 50:21).

The Power of Collective Wisdom

In guarding the flock, the elder must confront false teachers, correct members caught in false doctrines, expose sinful behavior, hold tightly to righteousness in the midst of moral drift, and at times implement church discipline. It should not be surprising that every reference to appointing elders in the New Testament shows "elders" in the plural. We need the wisdom and support of each other. This protects us as well as the church. In the Old Testament there were the "seventy elders" (Exodus 24:9), and later, the "company of the prophets" (2 Kings 2) that served as a distinctive plurality of spiritual leaders.

In Acts 20:17, Paul asked to meet with the elders of the Ephesian church. It is evident that he intentionally invested in these leaders over a substantial period of time. Always the missionary, Paul spent more time in Ephesus (three years) than in any other church planting. So, when he tells these leaders to be on their guard and watch over the flock, there is a certainty that this is a divine plan. It is not at all difficult to see the wisdom in having more than just one person watching the church. Also, when an imperfect group of people are having trouble, what is more reassuring than a collective prayer and "think tank" composed of spiritual shepherds who can utilize their combined years of serving God? Even if the individuals in the body of elders would have considered their history as ordinary, or even mistake-laden, God has a way of using our past and our mistakes to his advantage and glory—and he helps us to gain wisdom in the process (Romans 8:26–32; 1 Timothy 1:12–14).

Many an elder has expressed gratitude for the fact that together they can collectively benefit from stories of what not to do, as well as tales of best practices and victorious blessings. It is in this context that one can see how a body of elders reflects God's design for the church's protection.

One final consideration is the call for the overseer to warn God's people (Ezekiel 33). If elders are expected by God to take a stand in the face of difficulty and possible resistance, then the body of elders is the Lord's support system to ensure strength. God and his Son are aware of human nature and our propensity to fear and to shrink back (Hebrews 10:38–39). Thus, he instituted the "buddy system" in evangelism (Mark 6:6–13) and in shepherding. Our God is consistent. His design is wondrous, and the elder's task the greatest honor.

Chapter Twelve

Every Effort for Unity

Darren Gauthier, Israel Ereola and Wyndham Shaw

As a prisoner for the Lord, then, I urge you to live a life worthy of the calling you have received. Be completely humble and gentle; be patient, bearing with one another in love. Make every effort to keep the unity of the Spirit through the bond of peace. There is one body and one Spirit, just as you were called to one hope when you were called; one Lord, one faith, one baptism; one God and Father of all, who is over all and through all and in all. (Ephesians 4:1–6, emphasis added)

Disciples are to make every effort to gain and maintain unity. "Every effort" not only includes physical effort such as time and travel, but also includes effort in our character growth. Paul, in Ephesians 4, states essential ingredients for unity: humility, gentleness, patience, and love. To create and maintain unity, elders must possess and grow in these qualities. We cannot be ministers of reconciliation and fail to make every effort toward unity.

Unity is sweet. Unity is pleasant. Psalm 133:1 reminds us, "How good and pleasant it is when God's people live together in unity!" We have experienced the beauty of this harmony, and we have most likely experienced the discomfort of disunity. So how do we make every effort to maintain unity?

Unity Builders

Unity, like everything else, does not happen by accident. It must be forged and maintained—the same as in our physical families. What are some practices that help build unity in our families? Some of the most important practices we have learned include:

Shared convictions. The Bible must be the basis for our convictions. Otherwise, deep unity in mind and thought can't be maintained.

Shared vision. What do we want our family to be? What do we want to be known for? How can we work together toward this end? We need to build with our aim in mind.

Time together. It's impossible to build or keep unity without spending time together. These times include meals and both difficult and enjoyable, fun experiences.

Prayer. There is truth to the saying, "The family that prays together stays together." Prayer unites our hearts toward one God and one purpose. Prayer connects us with God and each other.

Vulnerability. We have learned that opening our lives to each other is the only way to build closeness. Without openness, we can't really know each other even if we are around each other. Vulnerability builds safety, which contributes to unity.

Laughter and tears. Sharing joy and laughter helps build unity. Joys and celebratory events are much less satisfying when not shared. Also, sorrow, grief and tears draw us together. Unity comes through shared emotions as we "show up" to share them.

Listening. Unity is built through truly hearing each other's thoughts, fears, questions, doubts, and troubles. Unity is built through listening to spoken and unspoken words.

Encouragement. Families unite when the members of the family encourage each other. Without this, we can become disheartened, discouraged, and disenfranchised.

Forgiveness. Family members are sure to hurt each other at times. Forgiveness is vital. Lack of forgiveness and bitterness will kill unity.

How do we implement these in the church and with each other? We must practice them. We must model them. We must grow in them. We must teach them. We must be steadfast and earnest in our effort to make progress in all unity-building processes.

Unity Busters

Of course, Satan will try his best to create disunity. He knows that if he is able to divide us he wins many battles. He also knows (consider the Babel tower) that when those who follow God are united nothing is impossible. Since Satan is always seeking to destroy, challenges constantly and consistently arise that make it difficult to achieve lasting unity. What are some obstacles that seek to destroy unity?

Unity busters include:

Hesitation. Most of us don't like to engage in conflict and can hesitate to address disunity. Elders must be men of courage who don't shy away from conflict. Paul made sure that unity was addressed (even if he could not do it himself), as illustrated by his insistence that the problems between two beloved sisters in the church (Euodia and Syntyche) be addressed (Philippians 4:2).

Making assumptions without hearing both parties. Too often we can be tempted to have a preconceived conclusion as to the guilt of a party. Every effort means we take time to hear both sides of a conflict (Proverbs 18:17).

Treating disputable matters as doctrine. Elders must understand that some points of view are neither right nor wrong, but matters of opinion. We must learn the art of unity in diversity.

Failure to bring matters to resolution. If we leave matters unsettled, they will calm for a time but then burn again. Ron Susek's excellent book, *Firestorm: Preventing and Overcoming Church Conflicts*,[10] addresses this principle. Resolution involves an understanding of the hurt or wrong done, a stated apology and request for forgiveness, and a commitment to approach the matter differently in the future.

Favoritism and racism. This includes insufficient understanding and acceptance of differences in tradition, as well as cultural and environmental influences. Elders are charged to direct the affairs of the church without partiality or favoritism (1 Timothy 5:21). We must be willing learners of cultural influences and traditions important to those from different backgrounds, and honor one another above ourselves (Romans 12:10).

Dysfunctional communication. Conversations (written and spoken)

---

[10] Ron Susek, *Firestorm: Preventing and Overcoming Church Conflicts* (Grand Rapids, MI: Baker, 1999).

can unite or divide. We find it helpful to ask questions before making statements, express warmth, speak in a tentative manner (when the situation does not call for a rebuke), and feel with or empathize with the hearer. We will share more ways of making every effort for unity in crucial conversations in the section "Every Effort in Our Words."

Allowing bitterness or lack of forgiveness to remain in the church. Those who are unwilling to forgive won't receive God's forgiveness (Matthew 6:15). How important it is to call to repentance those who are unwilling to forgive! If elders don't, who will? God sees forgiveness as urgent (Matthew 5:23–24). If allowed to persist, a root of bitterness will grow and defile many (Hebrews 12:15).

Pride and unwillingness to submit to one another. Philippians 2 describes the attitude of Jesus we are all called to have. If we desire to be right more than to understand, we will not make every effort to maintain unity. Unity begins with humility. Our humility should be obvious to others, including a willingness (no, eagerness) to state when we are wrong or need to apologize ourselves.

All these breakdowns can derail the ministry and become barriers to the spiritual health and growth of the church. Elders must work toward solutions.

In Acts 6:1–2 the apostles encounter a problem creating disunity. Grecian Jewish widows were being overlooked by the Hebraic Jews. The Twelve sought a creative solution that addressed the problem at hand. While they could have simply asked for apologies, they went beyond the immediate issue to find ways to overcome the problem.

The unity builders and busters not only apply to disciples in the church but are also imperative for creating unity within the leadership.

Leadership Team Unity

Elders play a powerful role in the unity of church leadership. A united leadership inspires the entire church to join together for one purpose, while a disunited leadership will stall and discourage church health and growth. Leadership in the church must be united in biblical convictions and vision for the church. In matters of opinion, respect for the views of others is essential. If we believe our opinion is always the right one, we will become a barrier to unity.

What does it take to build and maintain unity among leaders? The exact same qualities for building unity in the family and in the membership are needed to make every effort to create and sustain unity in the leadership.

Leaders must remember the common goals of the leadership mentioned in Ephesians 4:12–13: "to equip his people for works of service, so that the body of Christ may be built up until we all reach unity in the faith and in the knowledge of the Son of God and become mature, attaining to the whole measure of the fullness of Christ."

If leaders are concerned for personal status, are overly sensitive, or fail to respect other's opinions, they are at great risk for Satan's attacks on unity. Also, if leaders are exhausted or lacking a closeness with God they (we) are vulnerable and at risk for disunity.

As elders, part of our work within the leadership may include creating clear role definitions and a healthy structure for accountability in those roles. Unified and clarified working environments are good and pleasant.

Make Sure God Is in "Every Effort"

"Every effort" is not passive, but effort involves more than *our* work. It is imperative that we *first* invite God into all situations, remembering that his Spirit is in us. His Spirit is the ultimate producer of unity. We can be tempted to "fix" situations without first going to God for his partnership and blessings in our efforts. It is the Spirit of God who grants repentance (2 Timothy 2:25). We must make every effort to bring God into our relationships and must call on those involved to do the same. Our efforts won't substitute for his. We certainly have not made every effort to maintain unity without significant prayer and fasting (Mark 9:29).

Every Effort in Our Words

James 3:5–8 teaches us the power of the tongue. It can light a fire and is full of poison. Elders must to be excellent communicators.

If you're like most people, scarcely a day passes that you don't face a difficult conversation. You know the type—stakes are high, opinions vary, and emotions run strong. Below are eight tips extracted from the bestseller *Crucial Conversations* by Kerry Patterson and Joseph Grenny, designed to turn crucial conversations into experiences that produce strong results and build relationships.

These tips ask the questions:

1. *When do I need a crucial conversation?*

Anytime you're stuck—when a professional or personal relationship goes into a rut, or you're having trouble achieving results in your team or organization—ask "What conversations are we not facing or not facing well that are keeping us stuck?" *A Crucial Conversation will help both parties break through to new levels of understanding and commitment.*

2. How do I stay focused during a crucial conversation?

Before entering your crucial conversation, ask, "What do I really want for me? What do I really want for others? What do I really want for the *relationship?" The clearer you are about your goals, the less you'll be controlled by your fears.*

3. *How do I catch warning signs of trouble before it's too late?*

When others move to silence (withdrawing, masking, avoiding) or violence (controlling, labeling, verbally attacking), these are signs that others don't feel safe. Learn to look for silence or violence—signs that safety is at risk. *When crucial conversations turn ugly, the problem is not too much candor, it's too little safety. With enough safety, you can talk about anything.*

4. *How do I make it safe to talk about anything?*

People don't get defensive because of the content of what you're saying. They get defensive because of the intent they perceive behind it. When others become defensive, stop talking about the issue and clarify your purpose. *Help them understand your motives by sharing what you really want out of this conversation for you, for them, and for the relationship (see #2).*

5. *How can I master my emotions?*

Master your emotions by getting to their root. We make ourselves upset during crucial conversations when we 1.) cover up or ignore our role in creating the problems we're discussing and 2.) exaggerate others' role in the problems by attributing the worst possible motive to them. *Ask yourself 1.) What am I pretending not to know about my role? and 2.) Why would a reasonable, rational, and decent person do what the other person is doing?*

6. How can I be persuasive but not abrasive?

Start with the facts. Instead of launching with your emotions, begin by sharing the facts. Describe the concrete and objective experiences (what others said or did—not what you think about what they said or did) that created your concerns. For example, start with "In the meeting you referred to the proposal as 'My idea.'" Don't start with "You backstabbing jerk, you took complete credit for our proposal in there!" *When you start with your facts, you help others see how a reasonable, rational, and decent person would think and feel as you do. When they come to this realization, it is harder for them to become defensive at even the most controversial things you have to say.*

7. How can I explore others' views?

The easiest way to reduce defensiveness? LISTENING. Spend as much time exploring how others see the issues as you spend sharing your own. *Exploring* means that you are genuinely curious about others' views. Your goal is not necessarily to agree with them, but instead to discover how a reasonable, rational, and decent person would think and feel as they do. *The more curious you become, the safer others will feel and the less likely you are to get hooked by what they say.*

8. How can I end it well?

End with clear expectations. Don't be satisfied with just a good talk. Move to action by ensuring that everyone is crystal clear about how to get the issue resolved once and for all. Come to specific agreement about who is going to do what by when. Then agree when you'll follow up to see that you and others have kept these commitments. *Clear agreements and disciplined accountability turn great conversations into great results.*[11]

---

[11] Kerry Patterson, Joseph Grenny, John McMillan, Al Switzler, *Crucial Conversations: Tool for Talking When Stakes Are High* (New York: McGraw-Hill, 2012).

Every Effort in Resolving Personal Differences

Personal differences among disciples require immediate action. The action first involves directing the parties to properly adhere to the biblical steps of resolution. If this does not work, the Scriptures instruct them to bring in outside help (Matthew 18:15–17). Either way, these matters should take high priority before they begin to spread through rumors and misinformation, causing confusion and disharmony among members. While Scripture gives each disciple a clear process toward resolution, the elder must ensure that this process is working. Resolutions have a greater chance to emerge through one-on-one discussions and prayer. However, when the process breaks down, the elders are there to facilitate further discussions to ensure that every effort is being made to bring unity.

Every Effort Between Leaders and Disciples

Sometimes disunity occurs between leaders and the disciples they are leading. Resolution requires hard work and careful thought, as this type of disagreement can potentially have far-reaching and negative impact. Trust of leaders by the disciples (and the members by the leaders) is essential to a heathy church environment. These relational difficulties can be nuanced and require a balanced approach.

Again, Scripture provides guidance, and it is up to the elders to call all parties to a wholehearted devotion to God's word. One of the difficulties with this relational issue is the possibility for favoritism, whether real or simply perceived (1 Timothy 5:21). However, the potential for this to arise is lessened by the prior efforts of the elders to know and express their love and compassion for the flock. In the end, the opportunity to get everyone reconciled and preserve the unity within the church is a blessing from God. This will require follow up and continued oversight, as the goal is *complete* unity.

Every Effort Among Leaders

The elders have the charge to resolve issues of disunity among all levels of leadership, which include all biblically appointed offices. Our goal is to facilitate continued cooperation that can remove work friction. Several kinds of friction among the various levels of leadership

may include:
1) An unhealthy, competitive environment
2) Insubordination
3) Negative reinforcement
4) Favoritism
5) Unfavorable performance
6) Neglect
7) Personal agendas

All of these temptations (and others) are reasons for the elders to be attentive to the dynamic among leadership. While it is impossible to entirely avoid conflict at this level, the efforts by the elders to promote love and good communication can significantly reduce the intensity and potential fallout of such conflicts. Unity is the force that translates vision into action and blesses the entire church family with a trusting and secure environment.

Every Effort Between the Staff and the Board

Smaller churches are likely more at risk for conflicts between the staff and the board, primarily because larger churches often have elderships. In our smaller churches, the role normally filled by the elders can fall to the board of directors. These are usually men and women in good standing within the congregation and well respected by the members.

While their input and wisdom is valuable, this role is more for legal purposes and is not a biblical office. The leadership team of one of these congregations without a functioning eldership would be wise to connect the congregation to one with elders. This can help all parties to work within the parameters of their roles, thus promoting unity through clarity and respect for specific functions.

It seems prudent for elders to provide consultation and training to those churches willing to accept such. The need for elders is one felt by every church, and any effort to fulfill that need can help promote unity throughout our families of churches.

In churches with established elderships, these conflicts can still arise. Preemptive teaching is essential for creating a cohesive culture that works through these disunity traps. While creation of and adherence to clearly stated and biblically based bylaws are necessary, previously defined clarity and understanding of authority and roles create preventive measures that help maintain unity. The elders would be wise to work closely with members of the board in order to optimize communication. Let's not be caught off guard by the disunity this type of conflict can create.

Every Effort in our Families of Churches

The elders of the churches that make up each regional "family of churches" must develop synergy to work together toward a common goal.

Members of families of churches may develop a healthy and unified understanding of function within the churches, and their common ideas may be written out and accepted by all. This can become a framework for each church applicable to all the member churches concerning commitment to spirituality and general worship practice. These core beliefs should be in accordance with the purpose and convictions of the global goals of the brotherhood.

Some stronger churches might consider "adopting" the smaller and younger churches for the purpose of healthy and respectful interactions with a view to maturing each other through regular visits, teaching, and financial and administrative support. Provisions may be made to allow for sharing leadership expertise as well as strategic church planning in the region. A unified effort by the elders within a regional family of churches can create opportunities to find and develop future elderships throughout the region. The sharing of ideas, best practices, and even challenges can forge a bond of unity that pleases God and benefits all the disciples.

Every Effort in the Brotherhood

The focus of the brotherhood should be based on Mathew 28:18–20, where our Lord Jesus Christ gave the command to all disciples to "go and make disciples of all nations, baptizing them in the name of the Father, Son and the Holy Spirit, and teaching them to everything I have commanded you."

While making every effort toward unity can tempt us to focus on the negative, we must remember that love covers a multitude of sin. Elders should be at the forefront in developing a culture of love in the church. One way we can make efforts toward unity is to be quicker to notice the good rather than being quick with our critiques. Let us be quick to appreciate each other's gifts, express appreciation, and outdo one another in showing honor.

In John 13:34 (NRSV) Jesus commands us:

> "I give you a new commandment, that you love one another. Just as I have loved you, you also should love one another. By this everyone will know that you are my disciples, if you have love for one another."

It is in obedience to this great command that our unity begins. As our efforts increase to save a lost world, the efforts to shepherd those saved souls as well as those leading the charge grows. The stakes are high. May we make "every effort" to keep the unity of the Spirit through the bond of peace.

120

Chapter Thirteen

ELDERS AS PEACEMAKERS: CONFLICT RESOLUTIONS
Walter Evans

"Blessed are the peacemakers,
for they will be called children of God." (Matthew 5:9)

"We're just going to be like the church in the Bible," was the common response of many in our fellowship who had left a traditional church background and found a vibrant faith of simple biblical Christianity. Yet, often when there was conflict within the church, or tension between those same brothers and sisters of faith, there would be dismay and unsettled confusion. "Why is this happening?" Or, "I thought we were living by the Bible and being like the church in the first century." At times I would be tempted to respond, "Have you *read* the Bible?" But then I resisted, realizing that no one likes conflict, and everyone expects the church not to have problems and "just get along." When we read that Jesus said, "In this world you will have trouble. But take heart! I have overcome the world" (John 16:33), we tend to think this should mean that when we left the world for Christ we left disagreement, misunderstanding, differences, strong opinions, and even stronger personalities.

Conflict Is Not New

No matter what translation you turn to or what version you prefer, within the pages of God's holy writ there is plenty of earthly conflict. Conflict between individuals, conflict between groups, and even conflict between highly respected and spiritual leaders who were used by God to do mighty deeds. Some might sigh and say that "at least when we get to heaven, we will have peace." I surely hope so, and I'm planning on it, but I reluctantly remind you that at one time, there was even war in heaven! (Revelation 12:7). Our expectation here on earth should not be to erase conflict from within the church or to establish rigid structure that locks everything down or shuts down church members who might disagree with each other (or even worse, members who disagree with the church leadership). No, our goal is to resolve conflict in a godly way, and biblical church elderships are God's mechanism to accomplish this goal. When opposing forces come together through spiritual mediation, God's glory is revealed and peaceful resolution and reconciliation are achieved. When this is the result, even the world around us will say, "God is truly in this place!"

Can Conflict Be Good?

Although we're reluctant to admit it, not all conflict is bad. By definition, conflict is *"competitive or opposing action of incompatibles: antagonistic state or action (as of divergent ideas, interests, or persons)"* —Merriam-Webster. In this definition we find various sides of an issue at odds with each other. As a conflict escalates, the issues will become more crystalized, and as that happens the picture will become clearer and more defined. It's often a painful process, but we learn that through the conflict, and many times as a result of it, we can make an informed decision. This is not in any way excusing sin and sinful behavior that may erupt during the conflict (more on this later), but at least we achieve enlightenment and information that enables us to move ahead. It is also noteworthy to see that conflict produces character. The disciple who refuses to be baited into sinful reactions during strong disagreements, while at the same time holding their ground on the issue at hand, is an example to many and stands aligned with the character of Christ. Lastly, conflict often does expose deeply rooted sin that needs to come out if true reconciliation is to be achieved. Very often the "issue" is not really the issue. It's only through difficult discussions that deeper hurts are revealed and a better course of reconciliation and true forgiveness can be achieved.

God's plan is perfect, and in that plan he's chosen to gather in heaven men and women from "a great multitude that no one could count, from every nation, tribe, people and language" (Revelation 7:9).

To be a part of that final and diverse gathering, we must have conviction about unity. Jesus spent his final hours on earth praying that we would be brought to "complete unity," so that "then the world will know…" (John 17:23). Jesus knew that keeping unity would involve hard-fought battles. We can't have real unity unless we are committed to dealing with conflict and value conflict resolution. We must no longer ignore issues that we know exist within our individual churches and even between our families of churches. We won't make it to that final glorious gathering of all God's people if our convictions aren't laser focused on godly resolution in our spiritual family.

Elders to the Rescue!

The need to deal with conflict is not unique to the church or to elderships. Everyday life is filled with challenging situations and numerous disagreements among those who get stuck over seemingly minor issues. Sometimes these issues get resolved and people move on, but often issues get "stuffed" and remain unresolved, or even worse, escalate into major battles.

Numerous men and women in and out of the church are conflict avoiders and live lives of quiet discontentment, suffering in silence. Others, if they don't stay silent, are often building their cases and forming a coalition of supporters that will help them fight for their cause. The ability to find outside sources that can navigate these choppy waters can be difficult, and there are professionals who offer their services with the hope of resolution. But the good news is that God has established biblical patterns that can be applied to Christians in conflict. He has also provided elders, who are uniquely qualified to help shepherd the opposing parties through the process.

As we examine 1 Peter 5:1–4, Titus 1:6–9, and 1 Timothy 3:1–7 we see qualities of elders that are needed in dealing with conflict. Let's identify the qualities of an elder and see how they apply to conflict resolution:

• **Life experience** – *faithful to his wife, children who believe, manages his own family well, children obey him, an example to the flock, blameless, a good reputation with outsiders*

These are all characteristics of a man who has put in the hard work to run the gauntlet of life. He has built a marriage and family as well as had an impact on those outside the church. You don't travel through these areas of life and come out successfully without knowing how to navigate opposition and deal with conflict. To quote a now-familiar insurance commercial, "He knows a thing or two, because he's seen a thing or two."

- **Balanced temperament** – *eager to serve, not quick-tempered, self-controlled, upright, temperate, gentle, not quarrelsome*

These character issues are prerequisites for an elder, ensuring his ability to step into a volatile situation and not let his emotions get in the way. He can be trusted by both sides of opposing forces to not let himself be swayed, and through his balanced approach he can often get both sides to compromise—giving up sacred ground for the common good. He doesn't need to be the hero in the end. Often, if the work is done well, most people, outside of the conflicted parties involved, are not even aware that a conflict has taken place.

- **Respected leader** – *a shepherd, is willing, blameless, an overseer who manages God's household, hospitable, disciplined, encourages others, able to teach sound doctrine, above reproach, respectable, not a recent convert, faithful*

Although we tend to classify leaders as those who are always up front and attract attention, often the elder is leading by living a godly life from the middle of the pack, with his life and family on display. Although opposing parties may at times disagree with his assessment, they can't take issue with his life and what he's allowed God to do through him. Elders are builders, too, and what they've built by the power of God gives them needed credibility amid difficulty.

Patience and More Patience

In addition to the biblical qualifications of an elder, it almost goes without saying that patience is paramount for the character of a shepherd. This much-needed fruit of the Spirit is especially important when warring factions are at odds in the church. In our quick-fix culture, many want one big meeting to solve all problems. This "one-and-done" approach rarely works with longstanding conflict. Usually weeks, if not months, are needed to gather information and make sure both sides feel heard. Many meetings may be necessary, and sometimes just when you think things are resolved there's an unforeseen setback. On occasion, others from outside the conflict looking in can give disparaging looks and seem to want to say, "Is that problem still going on?" An elder who gets frustrated or weary of the ongoing issue can often cause others to lose faith. Certainly there is a time to bring things to conclusion, but it usually takes longer than anyone would think. Elders need to be the ones who are in it for the long haul.

Practical Implementation

Although an elder must possess these biblical qualifications, this doesn't mean that he can't bring in outside resources and receive additional training. There are many useful courses in the areas of mediation and conflict resolution, as well as numerous helpful books. We have within our brotherhood disciples who are trained in these areas and can recommend classes that can be a great resource for more difficult situations. Scholastic support can be a tremendous addition, but we should always make sure that our baseline for resolution is grounded in Scripture rather than the latest ideas that come out of various schools of mediation.

It's a tremendous blessing to have an eldership within a church that is skilled at conflict resolution. But even when skilled elders are available, we must always be careful that we don't jump the gun or allow church members to come to the elders first when a situation arises. They need to first try to work it out on their own. Even though a shepherd has a heart for the sheep and wants to help when they are hurting, elders also need to be disciplined and not allow themselves to get drawn into a disagreement when the parties haven't made every effort to work things out by themselves. Matthew 18:15–17 is a common framework that is useful for bringing two parties together and helps to avoid more people taking sides when it's unnecessary. Too often, even in the most mature of churches, too many others get involved, or one party ignores the other in conflict and goes straight to the eldership with the problem. We have to realize that although it takes courage for the offended party to go to the brother or sister first, God's wisdom has proven time and time again that this alleviates most problems and keeps issues from escalating.

In some cases an elder needs to remove himself from a conflict because he is too close to the situation, won't be objective, and may react personally to the people involved. I find a touch of irony with the passage found in Acts 15 that shows Paul and Barnabas (along with the Jerusalem leadership) masterfully dealing with one of the thorniest situations in the early church, the issue of circumcision of the Gentile brethren. This is a terrific study in conflict resolution, and I admire the discipline and the use of process to reach a balanced conclusion that set a strong baseline for the early church. The irony is found later in the chapter as Paul and Barnabas have a conflict over a personal matter (family versus ministry) that results in them parting company. To see these two giants in the faith have victory over the big issue, only to dissolve their partnership over something much smaller, is perplexing until we realize that their conflict was personal. We should be aware that we cannot always see our personal biases, and consequentially we can muddy the waters and even slow down the reconciliation process because of them. Certainly this is one of the reasons that God always speaks of elders in the plural. Does a conflict feel too close to home? Let another elder take this one!

Types of Conflict in the Church

Most conflicts in the church that are in the latter stages can be resolved by the elders if time is taken, information is gathered, parties are (and feel) listened to, scriptures are applied, and there's no rush to judgment. Again, all efforts must be made to ensure that the opposing individuals have done everything they could to work things out, and they have adhered to a pattern such as the one in Matthew 18. Elders should be prepared to oversee various issues like the following:

- Marriage difficulties where divorce is being considered
- Members at odds with each other because of personality differences

- Members in disagreement because of leaders or full-time staff
- Members causing disunity among other members that could be considered divisive
- Members reacting because of standards and expectations that have been set by the leadership
- Staff at odds with one another
- Strong opinions about areas like worship, dating, money, and the like

The list goes on. It can be tempting to feel overwhelmed, especially if there is a young eldership. But if elders take the needed time and hold to the Scriptures, in most situations (with the help of the Holy Spirit) the conflicts can be resolved.

Extreme Situations

There will always be certain situations that require more attention, in which the local leadership needs to use extreme caution and an abundance of prayer. This may not happen often, but sometimes members in conflict take extraordinary steps and bring in outside legal support and even law enforcement. This may include situations involving divorce, child custody, child abuse, sexual abuse, or other serious charges. Each church leadership must determine how they will handle these extreme cases. Depending on the situation, it may be wise to carefully support both sides while at the same time protecting both and relying on the professionals to come to their own conclusions. Following a verdict, decisions can be made regarding how it will impact the local church. Tremendous patience and discipline are needed, as these cases can go on for months if not years. These situations often involve heart-wrenching issues that can drive a church toward division as they become public and everyone has an opinion and wants to take sides. It is during these extreme cases that elders may wish to get outside counsel from other elders or professional brothers and sisters in our fellowship. It is also imperative that the eldership stays unified and supports one another during these trying times.

Conflict Beyond the Local Church

In Joshua 22 we read the account of the Transjordan tribes who almost went to war with each other based on a misunderstanding and some major assumptions. Unfortunately, the history of Christianity is not much brighter—filled with division as one group breaks away from another, forming separate denominations (sometimes over issues that the average member doesn't even understand). Even in our own lineage the banner of autonomy has been waved—often not over serious matters of governance, but rather over petty issues where one group couldn't get something worked out with another. They then separate and don't talk to each other, while still holding to the same doctrines of faith. While it seems very clear that the churches in the first century appointed local elders that had authority over that church only, there was still a lot of cross-communication and a sense of brotherhood that kept churches linked together. We dare not hide behind the mask of autonomy simply to avoid conflict between one church and another. Very often this separation is a result of strong leaders who have gotten crossways with each other, and no one is stepping in to help. These sorts of conflict must be resolved, and it's the elders who need to push for reconciliation and unity. Certainly, individual churches will have their own style, personality, and differences of opinion—and of course, culture and region will always be factors to consider. We can be diverse and still be unified, but this will take great effort and a strong desire to stay united and resolved—refusing to choose the easy road of what some would call autonomy.

At the time of this writing, our family of churches is defined by thirty-four global regions. We have all praised God together during conferences as we joined together and witnessed his power. We have fellowshipped with brothers and sisters from all around the world, all unified but uniquely defined by our regional differences. There have been conflicts in the past between churches and even between regions in our global structure. Although no eldership claims to have any authority over any other church besides the local one that they serve, there have been efforts by the ICOC Elders' Service Team to help out with these conflicts when invited in by a particular church or region. Elders on occasion have gathered to discuss how to maintain unity and deal with conflicts in the Kingdom as they arise. Even now, we are discussing how we should resolve conflict in our family of churches when it goes beyond a local, or even regional level. No one wants to give any one group too much authority, but at the same time no one wants to see churches separate over unresolved difficulties. Satan's greatest weapon is always division, and we must be determined to fight disunity with all the spiritual strength and power at our disposal.

The eldership is one of God's greatest tools to deal with conflict within the local church and can also be the tool that helps our family of churches stay unified. We need to continue to build strong elderships around the world and see that they are biblically prepared and well trained to deal with conflict when it arises—in the home church or even in the churches worldwide.

> As a prisoner for the Lord, then, I urge you to live a life worthy of the calling you have received. Be completely humble and gentle; be patient, bearing with one another in love. Make every effort to keep the unity of the Spirit through the bond of peace. (Ephesians 4:1–3)

130

Chapter Fourteen

ELDERS AS COUNSELORS: WHEN DO WE RECOMMEND PROFESSIONAL TREATMENT

Dr. Mike Shapiro

Romans 15:14 implies that Christians are competent to counsel. In fact, encouraging others, giving advice, and offering counsel on spiritual issues appear to be among the God-given tasks of leadership in the body of Christ (Titus 1:9). However, if you've been a church leader for more than, say, five minutes, you have undoubtedly (while counseling somebody, on one occasion or many) heard that little voice in your head. You know, the one that whispers something like, *I'm in over my head or I am now officially above my pay grade.* Call it the voice of the Spirit or that of an angelic being, but ignore it at your peril! It is my belief that experienced leaders hone this instinct over their years in the ministry. To heed that voice is not a sign of failure, weakness, or incompetence. The very opposite is true: only the wisest and most competent counselors are willing to admit when the situation is beyond the scope of their experience or abilities.

How to Not Get in Over Our Heads

Before we talk about how to draw on mental health resources outside of the Christian community, let's try to quiet that voice by looking at some "land mines" that a church leader can avoid in order to prevent him from getting in over his head in the first place. The first of these has to do with roles. Yes, elders are called to counsel. I know of many elders who are excellent at spiritual counseling, because they are facile with the Bible, humble, and know to not lean on their own understanding (Proverbs 3:5). However, elders need to be clear about what is outside their purview. As an elder, you must make it plain that you are not the person's psychologist, psychiatrist, or therapist—instead, you are the shepherd of a church. While you have an individual responsibility to help the congregant spiritually, you also have a church (and your own reputation) to protect. Be very clear about the limitations of the help you can give. This will prevent misunderstandings and derail potential problems from the outset.

The next issue has to do with a concept called transference. This is a term coined by the most famous ancestor of my profession, Sigmund Freud, who noticed that some of his patients (many of whom were rich, bored Viennese women) had a tendency to redirect or project their feelings and needs onto him. For those who sought a father figure or compassionate lover, he became the object of their affection. For those who had been mistreated by men, he became the archetypal abusive father or husband.

Similarly, as a church leader who has considerable referent power (which is defined as a leader's ability to influence a follower because of the follower's loyalty, respect, friendship, admiration, affection, or desire to gain approval), you are always a potential target of transference. In other words, sometimes people with mental or emotional challenges can put so much focus on you that they end up blaming you for their ongoing difficulties.

Have you ever given a sermon or taught a lesson, after which you were greeted by an emotional tirade from a disgruntled member of the congregation? Whatever you said might have touched a memory or a repressed feeling, thereby triggering some transference within that person. As a father figure in the church, you may become every abusive father or alcoholic husband or dishonest boyfriend from that person's past. Don't take it personally, but also don't put yourself in a position to foster it. Again, keep your role and your boundaries clear.

Incidentally, because there are so many women in our congregations who have been emotionally wounded by men, it is this author's opinion that the whole prospect of men counseling women—at least without another woman present—is fraught with danger, mainly because of the potential for transference, both positive (e.g., a woman looking for an "ideal" man) and negative (a woman who has "trust issues" with men projecting that mistrust onto the well-meaning elder). Even more disconcerting is the potential for counter-transference in such situations. This is when the leader, therapist, or other referent authority projects his own needs back onto the congregant. No one is above this; most of us who have chosen lives of leadership have a "need to be needed." It is a recipe for disaster when, in response to a church member transferring her needs onto an elder, the elder (in response to his own perceived needs) reciprocates by trying to fulfill her need for a "hero" or an ideal man. This is how unhealthy and inappropriate relationships—sometimes in the form of extramarital affairs—are born.

How and When Can We Recommend Professional Help?

Hopefully, the previous paragraphs have spurred you to some introspection about how to know your limits when you offer counseling and spiritual advice to members of your congregation. If the aforementioned "voice" has only become louder and has convinced you that you need to urge one or more of your congregants to seek professional help for a problem that is beyond your training, role or expertise, how do you proceed? How do you wisely lead someone with mental health issues to get professional help, since this will mean sending them to a professional who may or may not share our convictions about God and the Bible?

Let me first say this: Thirty-five years as a psychologist has only made me more convinced that all answers are in the Bible. I was a psychologist for about five years before I became a disciple of Christ, and when I first read the Bible I was amazed to find that many modern psychological techniques were already in there. God seemed to know a lot about psychology.

For example, there is a therapeutic technique that is very popular nowadays, called Cognitive Behavior Therapy (CBT). It was "invented" in the 1950s and was initially referred to as Rational Emotive Therapy. The theory behind CBT is that your thoughts dictate your emotions, not the other way around. Consequently, the goal in CBT is to train the individual to recognize and change negative or erroneous thoughts, thereby precipitating a positive change in mood. As proud as we psychologists are of our accomplishments when it comes to "inventing" psychotherapeutic techniques, one need only read 2 Corinthians 10:5 ("Take captive every thought to make it obedient to Christ") or Philippians 4:8 ("...whatever is true, whatever is noble, whatever is right, whatever is pure, whatever is lovely, whatever is admirable—if anything is excellent or praiseworthy—think about such things") to realize that God was ahead of psychology by about 2000 years!

Another example is something called mindfulness-based therapy. This is a very useful technique that has a good deal of empirical support in the scientific literature as an effective, short-term therapeutic technique (in fact, insurance companies love it because of the "short-term" aspect). Mindfulness therapy teaches one how to pause, quiet the mind, live in the moment, get centered in the present, and not get upset by one's own past (which can't be changed anyway) or worrisome thoughts about the future. I believe that God had this in mind when he said, in Psalm 46:10, "Be still, and know that I am God." There's also Matthew 6:34, "Therefore do not worry about tomorrow, for tomorrow will worry about itself. Each day has enough trouble of its own." That is the essence of mindfulness in a few short and helpful scriptures.

So, the principles of truly effective psychotherapy have their foundation in Scripture. Sometimes, people with mental health issues just need some help in learning how to apply them. At other times, people need to have the symptoms of depression or anxiety brought under control with medication before they can possibly benefit from psychotherapy. With this in mind, how does an elder know when it's time for someone to seek professional help?

Of course, every individual is different, and every situation is different. Especially in the world of mental health, there are no one-size-fits-all solutions. Therefore, as Christians trying to help other Christians, you first need to pray for wisdom and discernment (as I do every day before going to the office) and try to exercise your best judgment, which has hopefully been sharpened by years in the ministry. Once again, there is something to be said for gut feelings. If you feel that someone needs help beyond what you or the church can give, you are probably correct. Here are some general guidelines and things to consider when counseling others to get professional help:

First, I should note that in the world of psychiatry, a problem is no more than a "normal" problem unless it interferes with "normal" social or occupational functioning. In other words, everyone gets depressed, and everyone gets anxious at times. However, in most cases, depression and anxiety are transient things that eventually dissipate and don't interfere with work, socialization, school, and so forth. If someone is having trouble just getting out of bed in the morning because of anxiety or depression, it may be time to refer. If someone's performance on the job is declining to the point that they are about to get fired, it may be time to refer. If someone has become unusually withdrawn, reclusive, or asocial, it may be time to refer. Lastly, if depressive or anxious thoughts are sufficiently severe to impede someone's ability to read the Bible, pray, attend church, and interact with brothers and sisters in the congregation, it may be time to refer.

I should note that these guidelines must be applied at the proper time. Once again, almost everyone experiences at least some of these symptoms at one time or another. However, in the world of psychiatry and psychology, a diagnosis is usually not made unless the symptoms have been present for more than three months (cf. the *Diagnostic and Statistical Manual of Mental Disorders,* now in its fifth iteration). This is to prevent the mental health professional from misdiagnosing something like a grief reaction following the death of a loved one, wherein it would be perfectly normal for someone to exhibit symptoms of depression and anxiety for months or even years.

Dealing with Suicidal Thoughts

At this point, we need to discuss the issue of suicidal thoughts and threats, which are among the most urgent and important "red flags" that should alert the church leader to the need to refer to a mental health professional. As a prelude to this, we need to make a distinction between various degrees of suicidal ideation, as suicidal thoughts are commonly called in the world of psychiatry.

Over the course of time, most people entertain thoughts of suicide in some form or another. In the midst of some prolonged crisis, be it family, financial, or physical, most people will entertain a passing thought like, "I wish I was never born," "I don't want to be here anymore," or even, "If this is the way it's going to be for the rest of my life,

I'd rather end it now." This kind of lament, which would certainly be considered normal in context, is referred to as passive suicidal ideation. It's comforting to discover that some of God's most spiritual prophets entertained similar thoughts. See, for example, Moses' reaction to stress (Numbers 11:10–15) and Elijah's despair when he was on the run from Jezebel (1 Kings 19:1–5).

In terms of severity, the next most distressing type of suicidal ideation involves the issue of planning or intent. There's quite a difference between a transient thought about the relief death would bring, and a more "active" thought wherein someone actually makes a plan to end his or her life. We in the mental health professions are always careful to try to distinguish the two through some gentle but probing questions to determine whether or not the individual has seriously considered harming him or herself and, if so, how? Does the person have access to the means to implement their plan?

Even though no one can read another person's mind, there are often some troubling behaviors (readily evident to the friend or family member) that reflect the inner turmoil of suicidal intent. For example, someone may busy her or himself with "getting affairs in order," quitting a job suddenly, or unexpectedly giving away personal possessions. There are also life-threatening behaviors such as habitually driving too fast, leaving home without telling anyone, and cutting oneself (a behavior that deserves its own book but will not be thoroughly considered in this chapter). An elder dealing with a troubled church member should always be on the lookout for such behaviors. However, it is almost proverbial in the world of mental health professionals that "the best predictor of future behavior is past behavior," particularly when it comes to suicide. So, anyone who has a history of suicidal or self-harmful behaviors should be considered at greatest risk for such behaviors in the future.

Regardless of the severity and extent of suicidal ideation, it must never be ignored. It must also be considered beyond the purview of the untrained church leader. In other words, suicidal thoughts and behaviors—regardless of whether they are passive or active—must never be trivialized, and the individual must be guided to a qualified mental health professional. How is this done?

"Do You Want to Get Well?"

First, it is good for elders to keep in mind that it's ultimately the individual's responsibility to get help, not ours. If an individual is not sufficiently motivated to take the ultimate steps to get help (calling to make appointment, vetting the qualifications of the clinician, and so forth), then attempts at help may be ineffective. I believe that Jesus was assessing the paralytic's commitment in this way when he asked, "Do you want to get well?" (John 5:6). If the individual is committed to seeking treatment and is willing to try and help him or herself, then the best use of our time is to help guide the person to the proper resources.

On occasion, it has been disconcerting to me to receive a call or an email from a church leader who is very concerned about the emotional well-being of someone under their care. The well-meaning church leader will brief me about the situation, and then ask to make an appointment for the person to see me. In such cases, I worry that the church member is being enabled by the church leader. In other words, the leader is making things so easy that the member has to exert very little energy to help her or himself. In my experience, such people do not have a good prognosis! They want other people to help them but are unwilling to put in the hard work to get well in the long run.

The person seeking help should at least call to make their own appointment, as this assures me that they are motivated to get help. As an elder, you can guide, give advice, help find a doctor or a therapist, and even drive the person to the appointment if necessary. However, we have to be sure that the church member is taking at least some responsibility for their own treatment. One who is not so motivated is at high risk for missing appointments, cancelling at the last minute, and otherwise "sabotaging" treatment before it even begins.

Once someone is committed to seeking help, it's time to go shopping. How nice it would be if the world were filled with countless disciples who are also trained mental health professionals, thereby making it easy to pick someone who is trustworthy and shares our same worldview. While this is just not the case, we can take comfort in the fact that God works through non-Christians to help those who are his children. Nevertheless, when seeking treatment in "the world," the term *caveat emptor* applies ("Let the buyer beware!"). We need to be informed consumers who know something about the kind of help being sought.

How Can We Direct People to the Right Kind of Professional?

First, for someone seeking mental health help, they will be quick to find that there are lots of different kinds of mental health professionals, with lots of different specialties and different levels of training. Let's try to sort them out by starting with the doctors.

Do you know the difference between psychiatrists and psychologists? About $80 an hour! (That joke never gets old and is guaranteed to remain in my arsenal for years to come.) But seriously, in the world of mental health professionals, those who are referred to as "Doctor" are either psychiatrists or psychologists. Psychiatrists are Medical Doctors (MDs) who have gone to medical school and have been trained to deal with medication. They are experts on how psychoactive drugs affect the human body and interact with other drugs. Usually, they act in concert with other mental health professionals. For example, they may manage a patient's medications, while psychologists or professional counselors take on their therapy.

In the realm of psychology we have people with doctorates in philosophy (PhD), education (EdD), or psychology (PsyD). Although these three degrees sound very different, they can all be licensed in their state as clinical psychologists who provide direct services to patients. Most psychologists have extensive training in psychotherapy. They can also perform psychological testing to ensure proper diagnosis of a mental illness. Depending on their training, some (such as yours truly) can also assess patients for developmental disorders, like learning disabilities, developmental delays, autism, and attention deficit disorders.

Lastly, there are many mental health professionals who are licensed at the level of a master's degree. At this level, there is an alphabet soup of professions: LPC (Licensed Professional Counselor), LMFT (Licensed Marriage and Family Therapist), and LCSW (Licensed Clinical Social Worker), to name some. These counselors and therapists are good at teaching techniques for healing or self-improvement, such as the aforementioned Mindfulness Therapy or Cognitive Behavior Therapy.

Once again, these three main types of professionals often work in concert: for example, a patient may see a psychiatrist who refers them to a psychologist for an evaluation, after which they are referred to a professional counselor for therapy. This may seem inconvenient, but (like the medical profession) the amount of knowledge necessary to treat many illnesses is just so great that no one mental health professional can "do it all."

I should mention that there are clinicians at all levels of training who specialize in treating children. This is important to keep in mind, because the treatment of young ones is a completely different world: most mental illnesses (for example, depression) look completely different in children than they do in adults. As such, the techniques for treatment are different, the tests used to make diagnoses are different, and (of course) the medications are different. Therefore, if someone is seeking help for a child, it is very important to ensure that the provider has been specially trained to deal with children.

Who Is the Best Person for the Job?

Now that you know something about the different varieties of mental health professionals, how does one go about finding a professional who is suited for the task? If word of mouth hasn't already led your church member to a good clinician, then a good place to start the search is in the office of their primary care physician (family practitioner or pediatrician). Since it is the job of the primary care doctor to refer patients to qualified specialists when necessary, they usually know who is good, reputable, competent, and qualified.

However, once a referral has been made, the one seeking help has the responsibility to vet the professional to whom they have been referred. I advise people not to be intimidated by all those degrees and diplomas. Call the psychiatrist, psychologist, or counselor. Ask if they have the training to deal with this particular problem. Ask about their education and licensure. Ask whatever you need to ask to feel comfortable about the person treating you. A relationship with a mental health professional is a little like a marriage: if there isn't some "chemistry" in the relationship, it may not work out. If the clinician is resistant to being "interviewed" or questioned about their training, then (to my mind) this is a sign of arrogance, and you should shake the dust off your feet. As a clinician myself, I have always welcomed the opportunity to answer any question from a prospective patient.

Hold Fast to Your Convictions

Finally, an important note about seeking help from non-Christian mental health professionals. The ethics of the professional licensing boards of all states, and the ethical codes of all the governing bodies of each profession (like the American Psychiatric Association, the American Psychological Association, and the American Association of Marriage and Family Therapists) uniformly declare that it is highly unethical for a mental health provider to impose their "worldview" onto the consumer.

In other words, even if the provider is a non-Christian, atheist, or pagan, they must be respectful of the client's feelings and opinions about the Bible. Therefore, at the outset of the therapeutic relationship, it is wise for the church member to inform the provider that she or he is a Christian who is seeking advice and help, but will NOT do anything that is contrary to the Bible (for example, if someone is struggling with same-sex attraction, there are some therapists who might advise that individual to "indulge" or "explore" homosexuality, which is the very thing the Christian is attempting to avoid!). Any ethical provider will be more than content with that caveat and will respect the client's wishes. However, the provider can't know where the boundaries are unless the Christian speaks out at the outset of treatment.

In over thirty-five years of practice and over twenty-nine years of being a Christian, it has become evident to me that the Lord works through doctors and medicines to heal those who are prayerful and faithful. Once traveling down the path of mental health treatment, the disciple has a responsibility to stay faithful, read the Bible, continue to pray, and comply with medical treatment when it is recommended. If you as an elder can help the Christian do these things, then you will be following in the footsteps of the Twelve, who were sent out to "proclaim the kingdom of God and to heal the sick." By God's grace, we will be able to wisely guide our members to receive the help they need.

Chapter Fifteen

ELDERS AS LEARNING LEADERS
Wyndham Shaw

If you are reading this book because you aspire to be an elder, you may be thinking by now—I can never do all of this!

Welcome to feelings common to all.

The good news is that God is full of grace and truth and allows us to grow and learn. In fact, as we rely on him in our weakness, he fills us with his strength (2 Corinthians 12:7–10). You already know more than you think you do, have learned from years of life experiences, and most important, are filled with the Holy Spirit.

Thank God he allows us to participate in his divine nature and grow from one degree of glory to another (2 Peter 1:4; 2 Corinthians 3:18). God will give us what we need, through his word, his promised wisdom, the power of his Spirit, and relationships that offer us wisdom and give us confidence by confirming the validity or inaccuracy of our gut feelings.

We will make mistakes, but as we learn, they will happen less often. Learning leaders are learning leaders because they are humble. If you feel you "have it all together," you lack humility.

I find that when I suggest to a man the idea of becoming an elder, his first reaction is often apprehension, or even fear. This can come from numerous sources, not the least of which is failure to realize and have confidence that God sees leadership as a noble ambition (1 Timothy 3:1). Paul desires for men to desire to become elders, according to his own writings. He is aware that people can respond to the gospel with both good and bad motives, but he never questions the need for willing leaders.

Some men have godly character and lack confidence, while others have confidence but lack godly character. The goal is to have both ingredients in the same man. Godly conduct comes from good judgment and discipline about principles, as well as emotional intelligence in implementing them. It requires growth in character, competence in thinking, and acting in harmony with God's heart and will. Bold and humble leadership is possible, but it generally comes from modeling the example of others, experiencing hard lessons, and praying often. We can learn from our own experiences and the experience of others—but we must be learners.

Age does not make one wise; learning from experience does. While "elder" implies age, it should also imply a learner's spirit. Disciple means student or learner. Elders should be a demonstration of this spirit. We must be determined learners—learning on purpose.

The outcomes of decisions we make also provide a learning curve for wisdom. Elders should be able to describe what they have learned from all decisions, especially from ones that don't go well.

I remember in the 2001 leadership crisis in our fellowship, it was helpful for me to enumerate what I learned. I prayed, meditated, read the Scriptures, talked to others, and read many books.

In 2010 our elders experienced another learning curve, different from what we learned in 2001 to 2003. Some of the helpful practices we implemented evolved from lessons learned from decisions that did not go well. Often these lessons were concerned with who should have been involved with the decisions, what the decisions needed to be, and when and how they would best be communicated. Other lessons we learned concerned a pendulum swing resulting in a lack of wholehearted devotion to the Lord and increased sin in the church. We had to learn how to respond to this situation as well.

Paul, as he writes to Timothy, states a principle of leadership growth. Growth requires diligence and wholehearted devotion on our part.

> Be diligent in these matters; give yourself wholly to them, so that everyone may see your progress. Watch your life and doctrine closely. Persevere in them, because if you do, you will

save both yourself and your hearers. (1 Timothy 4:15–16)

As the Scriptures teach, this learning curve comes from diligence in public reading, teaching, and preaching of Scripture, and wholehearted pursuit of growth.

Our progress will be evident. We and others should be able to see ways we have grown. We grow more when we go after certain needed areas of growth.

These are some of the common areas of learning curves I have experienced over the years and have needed to implement in my life:

- Speaking with gentleness, rather than with an angry or frustrated tone
- Overcoming fear of confrontation or of calling others to grow—especially other leaders
- Learning to be agreeable without being a people pleaser
- Learning to persuade and be persuadable
- Learning to be a warm and approachable leader
- Learning to be vulnerable and share weaknesses
- Becoming a better listener
- Overcoming fear of making mistakes
- "Over-policing" leaders or decisions
- Growing in supporting, helping, and encouraging less-experienced leaders
- Growing in courage to make difficult, unpopular decisions

Remember that we and others should see progress, not perfection. We are sheep too, but ones who have been around the pen a little longer and thus have more experience and knowledge that is useful to the other sheep. The stakes of learning are huge, as the Scriptures teach. Perseverance in doctrine and growing in our spiritual life affect our salvation—as well as that of others.

Several years ago while in Singapore attending a conference, Jeanie and I viewed a huge construction site from the window of our hotel room. The story of Singapore's history gives an inspiring vision of a work in progress. Fifty years ago the city was filled with poverty, chaos, and pain. Kicked out by its "motherland," Singapore was left to fend for itself. Lee Kuan Yew, who became prime minister, looked out at his impoverished, abandoned, and isolated city—and from his love and passion envisioned a nation of unity, strength, beauty, and excellence. Over fifty years later Singapore enjoys all of these and more. It's a vibrant, thriving, and beautiful city.

At times we may be tempted to look at personal weaknesses or shortcomings in God's church with disappointment or even disdain. Are you quick to see the deficiencies? If so, it is vital as an elder to gain the vision needed for progress and the love and perseverance to see it through.

May we be ever learning and always growing, remembering that we, too, are works in progress. Let us never lose God's vision for his beloved church.

If a physical city can be built with human leadership and willing volunteers, imagine what God can do through his Spirit to grow us to completion as together we help build the kingdom of God on this earth.

> I thank my God every time I remember you. In all my prayers for all of you, I always pray with joy because of your partnership in the gospel from the first day until now, being confident of this, that he who began a good work in you will carry it on to completion until the day of Christ Jesus. (Philippians 1:3–6)

Chapter Sixteen

SHEPHERDS SEARCH FOR LOST SHEEP
Wyndham Shaw

Five years ago most everyone within a hundred miles of my home had heard of Snappy. Snappy was a family's beloved Weimaraner that was lost in our town. His owners searched for him relentlessly, putting up hundreds of "lost dog" signs. They even flew in professional dog finders from other states. My wife tells me they made a Facebook page, "Find Snappy," for updates and sightings. (My wife still occasionally checks to see if he was found.) He is still sought after, though most of the signs have fallen off their posts and decomposed.

Do we have the same urgency and persistence to search for those who have wandered from the Lord as this family had for their beloved pet? A shepherd searches for lost sheep (Luke 15:1–7). God longs to see his children restored. They are family. Unattended, they are preyed upon and in all kinds of danger.

Urgency to Restore Lost Sheep

God does not forget his children any more than we would forget one of our children. In fact, his memory is better! God makes restoration of souls a focus of body life and of one-another relationships (Galatians 6:1–2; James 5:19–20).

When a disciple wanders, the stakes are high. They could quickly lose their relationship with God due to unrepented sin and loss of saving faith. They need to be reconciled and restored to God and the family of God (Isaiah 59:1–2; Romans 1:16–17; Hebrews 11:6). Restoration is urgent because of the stakes involved—facing God in judgment and being separated from him by sin and a hard heart (Hebrews 2:1–3; 3:6–14).

Satan desires to deceive and devour; thus he preys on the weak and the young (1 Peter 5:8–9; 2 Timothy 2:22–26). He also looks for opportune times to steal the faith of the "strong." While each individual who has left is responsible for coming back to a saved relationship with God (Ezekiel 18:30–32), just as they were responsible for leaving, they need shepherds who will help them find the way home. As the story of the prodigal son shows, restoration, not judgment, is the heart of our loving Father (Luke 15:11–32) and should be our heart too.

Characteristics of Biblical Restoration

Restoration may deal with two dimensions of lost fellowship. The first is helping someone restore their relationship with God, and the second is helping them return to fellowship with the other disciples (1 John 1:1–7). The order and degree to which these two dimensions are applicable will require discernment, but Scripture is clear: one must be reconnected with both to be righteous before God.

Since restoration is something any one of us could need, let us seek to restore those who are lost with gentleness and humility (Galatians 6:1–2). People tend toward two extremes in unrestored states. Some have hardened their hearts, while others are filled with shame and guilt. (Others may have a mixture of the two.) Both attitudes make restoration equally difficult. We need maturity to differentiate and effectively work with either or both.

Often restoration is needed because a Christian has gradually (and sometimes unknowingly) drifted and wandered due to their lack of spiritual alertness and maturity (Hebrews 2:1–3; James 5:19–20). Regardless of how one wanders away, it is dangerous to remain unrestored to fellowship with God or his family.

All disciples should desire and be eager to contribute to the restoration process with other disciples, but not all are equally qualified to completely help them back. Those with maturity, knowledge, and experience should be eager to help, with elders leading the way (James 5:19; Galatians 6:1–2). The issues and process for restoration can be complex and require sensitive communication and action. We can tend toward being overly sentimental or overly harsh. Every situation calls for discernment that takes into account the sin and history involved.

Restoration ultimately involves repentance, forgiveness, acceptance, and reassurance on the part of the different parties involved with the process. The one restored must have repented of the sins leading to separation from God and his church (2 Corinthians 7:8–11). The Lord is eager to forgive, and his spiritual family must extend forgiveness and grace that offers freedom from guilt and shame to the one restored (Isaiah 1:18–19). Fellow disciples must offer acceptance and reassurance that produce a release from fear, shame, and guilt, and result in a feeling that everything is "back to normal." God has no doghouses or probation (Genesis 50:15–21; Luke 15:25–32; 2 Corinthians 2:5–10).

Restoration not only brings joy, but it also brings a sense of progress in growth to the individual and the church (Luke 15; James 5:19–20). The ministry of reconciliation is truly fulfilled when we follow the heart of Jesus and participate in the mission, to his glory. Baptisms and restorations are equally valuable parts of the church's ministry. The latter may bring even more joy since more people tend to be attached to the one who is restored, and therefore are affected by both the loss and the return of a "lost sheep."

How Do We Do This?

Snappy's owners were urgent and persistent. How much more should we search for souls who have wandered?

Some of the actions my wife and I have implemented to help us put our good intentions into practice have included:

- A decision to make phone calls to those who have wandered and to ask if we could get together to talk
- A conviction to reach out specifically to our members' adult children who have left the faith, letting them know we care by initiating with them
- Setting aside a specific night to invite lost sheep into our home: on a particular night of the week (each week) we invited an individual or a couple over who had wandered. We often set these visits up weeks ahead of time. Over dinner we had wonderful conversations that frequently led

to open bibles, open hearts, and deep talks. We saw numerous souls restored just by making this one decision about a specific way to regularly use our time.

Practical Wisdom for our Restoration Ministry

Wisdom is gained through the Scriptures, the Holy Spirit, experience, training, and input from others. We need wisdom to help sort out the deep waters that often have left wanderers struggling over their heads and in need of help (Proverbs 20:5).

Always ask the wanderer what caused them to leave the church and/or the Lord—and really listen to the answer. Determine if the person sees themselves as having left both God and the church. Two issues may need to be wisely addressed:

1. When someone in the church who was involved in their life caused them to stumble.

2. Recognition that God does not accept us being reconciled to him without being reconciled to his church.

These two may be related but not properly comprehended. God holds each of us responsible for keeping our covenant with him regardless of difficulties and disappointments incurred from his people (Romans 2:5ff). This is a difficult but crucial understanding of God.

Leaders and fellow disciples can contribute to a person stumbling in their faith, and God will judge their responsibility in the matter (Ezekiel 34:10; Luke 17:1–5). While forgiveness is crucial in the sight of God, a person may choose (after they are reconciled) to relocate to another body of disciples and set of leaders (because of difficulties with trust) and still be faithful to God. But one may not choose to remain separated from functioning in the body of Christ and still remain faithful to God.

As we engage in individual conversations involving conflict with others, we must always practice Proverbs 18:17 and hear the other side of the case. We must gather balanced information before concluding what or who is right or wrong.

We must keep the conviction that both one's life and doctrine must be in keeping with God's will to be faithful to his covenant. This must be at the center of our restoration discussions. False teaching is very attractive when someone is hurt or responding to the pain of past experiences. God does not change the terms of our covenant because of the bruises or bumps incurred as we keep it. Our own desires can quickly emerge to replace God's word if we are not diligent (2 Timothy 4:1–5).

Be careful to place the response and responsibility for restoration between the individual and Jesus. Someone's return to the group from which they left is not essential (such as the same congregation, family group, or region) but return to Jesus (life and doctrine) and a place in his body is vital.

While we never want to lose urgency to help restore a wanderer whose heart has softened and who wants to come back, the timing must be up to the faith, heart, and choice of the individual. Timing should not rest on anyone else's timetable or motive (2 Corinthians 6:1–3, 11–13; Romans 15:2–3). One's faith must increase to the point where they are ready to make a personal decision.

Bible study and prayer should accompany the entire restoration process—as both individual and joint ventures (Romans 10:17; 1 Corinthians 3:6–7).

As a person begins to express the desire for restoration, it is important to discuss the fruit of repentance that should be evidenced in their life (Luke 3:7–15). Sometimes people need help determining what repentance should look like. Jesus helped people understand this as he spoke with them about repentance. It is important to note the difference between ongoing repentance in the life of a disciple and the need for restoration.

A Time for Rejoicing

The Bible makes it clear that restoring a lost sheep is an occasion for as much rejoicing as losing one is for concern. We must ask God to keep both emotions within our spiritual capacity, especially over time as all phases of spiritual reality are no longer novel. We are called to never grow weary in doing good (Galatians 6:9). This will take the

Spirit's power and the love that God continually pours into our hearts. Jesus keeps fresh perspective and eager anticipation in each of our conversions or restorations. He is eager to initially save us by his grace and eager to keep the grace flowing. We must imitate his heart.

Conclusion

We must embrace a ministry of reconciliation that includes both the commitment to ongoing evangelism and the ministry of restorations. This need is particularly great when a church becomes large and has been around a long time, with successes and failures in reaching out to and shepherding souls. We must maintain a course of faith, action, and Christlike heart and spirit as we persevere in following Jesus.

May we help many find their way home to the glory of God.

> "I tell you that in the same way there will be more rejoicing in heaven over one sinner who repents than over ninety-nine righteous persons who do not need to repent." (Luke 15:7)

Chapter Seventeen

ELDERSHIP APPOINTMENTS
Wyndham Shaw and Al Baird

There are currently about fifty-nine elderships in the ICOC fellowship with around two hundred ten elders represented. This means only ten percent of our churches currently have mature models of church oversight and shepherding in place. Of these elderships, we would estimate that more than half have existed for less than five years.

Numerous elders were appointed between 2003 and 2005, a time when our church was experiencing a crisis. Many men with ministry and leadership experience were under fire and were marginalized. Leaders who had the most experience in shaping a clear conceptual, functional, and relational foundation for elderships were among those marginalized, creating a divide between evangelists and elders. This was often in response to our previous evangelist-led model of leadership. The reaction to this model transferred authority from evangelists to elders. Reactionary decisions often prevailed over learning from each other. Remnants of this divide still exist today, complicating the way biblical roles can function together in a unified and effective way.

At times men were appointed as elders during our "firestorm" period without inclusion of trained ministry leaders. As a result, some congregations suffered more division and longer decline. Training and experience in church building should not be replaced by elders who meet qualifications but lack seasoning in the crucible of leading people—we need both.

Knowing this, our congregation sought to appoint elders who were already leading in some capacity—such as in small groups or on leadership teams. Elders should not be novices to leadership and should always be involved in the basic tenets of discipleship.

Common Elements in Elder Development

We need a thoughtful plan for raising up elders and can learn from models of elder development in other churches. Our models don't have to be exactly alike, but they do need to be shaped by these common elements:

Biblical foundation: Scriptural principles must be the foundation for all we do. These principles must supersede personality, pragmatism, results, or appearances. Principles can be evaluated in terms of their truth and can be passed on. Personalities and results cannot be evaluated in this way.

Historical lessons: We are not the first or the best at attempting to build churches, but we can be some of the best at learning as leaders. As we study church history, restoration history, and our own history we can learn from previous victories and defeats.

Cultural implementation: Paul became "all things to all people" to win as many as possible. We must learn the "art" of applying Bible principles in different settings without violating or compromising revealed truth.

Form and function: Leaders decide which forms are best used to effectively accomplish biblical functions. Evangelism, prayer, one-another relationships, and worship are all biblical functions. How we practice these, individually and collectively, is left to the judgment and choice of leadership (Hebrews 13:17; 1 Thessalonians 5:12). Responsibilities for leadership and followership must be communicated. Forms can and should change based on culture and effectiveness, but functions should not change because they are based on absolute biblical principles.

Community theology: We can overcome the tendency to struggle in our leadership development and function by giving needed forethought and attention to our formation and application of biblical principles. Our leadership must have common convictions of Bible principles, historical lessons, cultural tendencies, and pragmatic forms for function together. Commonly held doctrines and practices of cooperation agreement provide good examples of this within the brotherhood. In our opinion, the more community theology we practice and agree on, the more united we will remain. In Boston this was the basis for the elders' decision on our understanding of "believing children" and eldership. Our elders and evangelists agreed together. Our community theology offers a basis for those coming in to be persuaded and understand for themselves, or persuade us to change it.

Identifying and Raising Up Elder Candidates

In the ninety percent of our churches without elders, we must raise up men qualified not only in character but in competence at overseeing and shepherding the mission and church-building process. This requires ongoing training for aspiring elders and their wives, and a clearly defined appointment process to ensure congregational support and followership.

Effective governance is not established merely by the appointment of elders. Competence, chemistry, clear decision making, and functional processes are crucial within the group. These can be learned through mistakes in the "school of hard knocks" or through a more encouraging blend of "what not to do" combined with the experience of others in conceptual, functional, and relational dynamics. The following are needed avenues for elder development:

Ongoing training and mentoring for eldership growth

Like new parents, company owners, and team coaches, new elders and elderships (and their wives) need mentors, resources, and education from those who have been in the trenches and have learned from biblical concepts and church experience. The most likely source of such training and development comes from those who have the most experience, have demonstrated a learning curve of increasing success, and can be accessible to teach others.

Creating unified teams

We also need to develop a unified team of gifted leadership roles that values and coordinates the contribution of all gifted roles, especially those of teachers, evangelists, and elders as suggested in Ephesians 4:11–12. A cord of three strands is not easily broken. We must braid them together so they can become the ties that bind us together.

Effective Selection and Appointment

Perhaps you have been identified as an elder candidate, or your church has identified candidates. Now what?

There is no exact formula for appointment, but the Bible does state that proposed elders need to be approved by the congregation for a time. The actual time frame for communication with the congregation and communication with the candidates and their families should be discussed and decided upon before beginning the process. It should be clear from the current leaders who is a true candidate and who will appoint them. Clarity of purpose and process brings a harmonious execution of plans.

Gordon Ferguson, who served as an elder in the Phoenix church, shared an account of the appointment process in the church there:

When elders were first appointed in the Phoenix church, principles found in the epistles were applied. Here were the steps: First, three sermons were preached on the biblical role of elders, the elder's family, and the selection and appointment process. Afterward, printed outlines of the lessons were handed out and were also posted on the church website. Then a meeting was held, open to anyone in the congregation who wished to attend, where any questions people still had about eldership were answered.

The church members were asked to participate in the selection process in the following ways:

- They were asked to pray that God would guide the whole process.
- They were asked to study the biblical qualifications of elders.
- They were invited to suggest names of men that they believed to be biblically qualified and judged to be good shepherds of the flock. (Forms were provided for this and

an end date was given for their submission.)

After this, the evangelists were very involved in making the final decision about who was to be appointed an elder. The remainder of the process of selection and appointment was as follows:

- The existing congregational leadership group, comprised of the evangelists and mature non-staff brothers, met to consider the names recommended.
- The men who seemed to be biblically qualified were contacted and asked if they wanted to be considered as elder candidates.
- The final group of elder candidates was selected and informed of their selection, and then the church was informed of the names.
- The members were invited to register any concerns that they had about any of the men whose names were put forward.
- An elder training class was started immediately, with two goals in mind: to determine which of the elder candidates should be appointed first; and to provide further training for all of the candidates.
- Finally, the first group of elders was appointed by the evangelists as soon as it seemed appropriate (several months after starting the training class).

The selection and appointment of elders is a crucial yet complex topic, without easy answers. The Bible does not spell out clear answers on every question, and so we must do our best to make decisions based on sound theology and biblical interpretation. This chapter has not answered all the questions that could be addressed—perhaps it's brought up questions you didn't know you had—but I hope we have provided enough information to be genuinely helpful. Where we lack explicit command or explanation in the Bible, may God guide us all to make the best possible decisions with the information we have. We highly recommend that you seek input from mature leaders outside your own congregation. God designed the church to be overseen by mature leaders, and may he guide us as we seek out, train, and appoint such men.

The Candidate Interview

In Boston, as we add to our eldership we find it helpful to have an "interview" with the candidates and their families. This involves dinner at their house with two elder couples and the region leader couple (where they live and serve) for the purpose of visiting in their home environment and discussing their desire for the role as well as the expectations involved.

Conversations have included:

- Spiritual history
- Family history
- Desire for the role from the husband and wife's perspective
- Biblical vision of the role in terms of character, family, dealing with difficult people, and upholding biblical standards in the church
- Their vision of an elder/eldership
- Dialogue of role expectations/schedule
- Explanation of the selection process
- Questions and answers
- Prayer together

Including the Family in the Process

In a second meeting we like to have a discussion that includes the elder's children (not necessarily in the same setting). The discussion would include:

- Asking them (without parents present) how they feel about their dad being an elder: what is their understanding, what is their view of his qualification, and do they feel any

pressure or burden for them as a son or daughter?
- Asking both spouses about the other's qualification and main strengths and weaknesses
- Asking spouse and children (in a setting without the candidate) if there is any reason they believe this should not occur at this time
- Preparing them for feedback from the congregation and the need to answer questions as part of the process
- Discussing the difference of being a candidate versus being appointed
- Explaining the next steps in the process
- Question-and-answer time

Eldership Models: Boundaries and Responsibility

We have both rejoiced as we have been part of elder training and appointments in various places throughout the world. Elders are needed in every culture and every nation. We have seen elders appointed in Lagos, Milan, Munich, Hong Kong, Toronto, Sydney, Melbourne, Paris, London, Buenos Aires, Kiev, and most recently Mexico City.

While more and more disciples in our churches are reaching or have reached the age to be appointed as elders, too few have been given a vision and process to become competent and confident at the personal or congregational level. Others find themselves stuck in patterns of dysfunction that can be felt and recognized but not overcome. I am aware of several congregations recently seeking outside counsel and input on both the path to appointing new elders and the process of developing better effectiveness at the conceptual, functional, and relational levels of existing elderships. Some obstacles to eldership development include:

The absence of experienced champions and educational materials. We need champions who have demonstrated success in the areas essential to effective church oversight. These areas include church growth (numerically and financially); unity of multiple leadership roles such as teachers, evangelists, and elders; and consistency in raising up and training new leaders by the existing ones—who go on to successfully lead at home and in other contexts.

The lack of training workshops and seminars. These are essential for evangelists and for those aspiring to be elders who need help from those who have more successfully navigated this matrix of leadership dynamics.

The lack of availability of men and women with experience and expertise to travel and provide training on mission fields that are even younger than the planting churches.

The absence of recognition and initiative from elders and elderships who need training and discipling to reach their full potential and be their best for God.

A lack of trust that training and influence can be passed on from outside sources without sacrificing authority or control in the local church.

A Bright Future

Despite the obstacles, more and more leaders are being raised up as our members age and mature. When we began writing this book the first sentence read, "There are currently about forty-five elderships in our fellowship with approximately eight-five elders represented." Today, with fifty-nine elderships and two hundred and ten elders (and counting), this means that in a short period of time many more elders have been appointed.

We long to see the scripture in Acts 2:17–21 continuing to be fulfilled.

> "In the last days, God says,
>   I will pour out my Spirit on all people.
> Your sons and daughters will prophesy,
>   your young men will see visions,
>   your old men will dream dreams.
> Even on my servants, both men and women,
>   I will pour out my Spirit in those days,

>   and they will prophesy.
> I will show wonders in the heavens above
>   and signs on the earth below,
>   blood and fire and billows of smoke.
> The sun will be turned to darkness
>   and the moon to blood
>   before the coming of the great and glorious day of the Lord.
> And everyone who calls
>   on the name of the Lord will be saved."

As the young gain vision for God's church, may the "old" never quit dreaming of all God can do with and for and by men who are fully consecrated to him.

For additional books go to
www.ipibooks.com

Printed by Libri Plureos GmbH in Hamburg, Germany